D1709403

The Crusades
Primary Sources

The Crusades
Primary Sources

Written by J. Sydney Jones
Edited by Marcia Merryman Means and Neil Schlager

U·X·L

An imprint of Thomson Gale, a part of The Thomson Corporation

Detroit • New York • San Francisco • San Diego • New Haven, Conn. • Waterville, Maine • London • Munich

The Crusades: Primary Sources

Written by J. Sydney Jones

Edited by Marcia Merryman Means and Neil Schlager

Project Editor
Julie L. Carnagie

Permissions
Lori Hines, Susan J. Rudolph, William A. Sampson

Imaging and Multimedia
Lezlie Light, Mike Logusz, Kelly A. Quin

Product Design
Pamela Galbreath, Jennifer Wahi

Composition
Evi Seoud

Manufacturing
Rita Wimberley

3 1218 00387 2513

LIBRARY OF CONGRESS CATALOGING-IN-PUBLICATION DATA

The Crusades. Primary sources / written [i.e., compiled and edited] by J. Sydney Jones; edited by Marcia Merryman Means and Neil Schlager.

p. cm. – (The Crusades reference library)

Includes bibliographical references and index.

ISBN 0-7876-9178-X (alk. paper)

1. Crusades–Sources–Juvenile literature. I. Jones, J. Sydney. II. Means, Marcia Merryman. III. Schlager, Neil, 1966- IV. Series.

D151.C767 2004
909.07–dc22
2004018001

Printed in the United States of America
10 9 8 7 6 5 4 3 2 1
ISBN 0-7876-9178-X

Contents

Reader's Guide

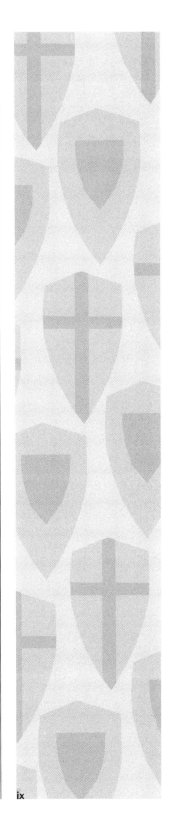

The term "crusade" is commonly used today to refer to a dedicated, enthusiastic effort. It usually means a total, all-out attempt to correct a problem, such as combating drunk driving or saving an endangered species from extinction. When people use the word "crusade," though, they may not recognize its distinctly religious meaning and history, even though they might embark on their crusade with religious enthusiasm.

The "Crusades" (with a capital "C") were a series of military campaigns launched by the Christian countries of western Europe in the late eleventh century. During these battles tens of thousands of people went to war in the Middle East. Their goal was to recapture the Holy Land, or Palestine, from the Muslims and restore it to Christian control. The focus of the Crusaders was the holy city of Jerusalem, now part of the Jewish nation of Israel on the eastern shore of the Mediterranean Sea and still a holy site to three religions: Judaism, Islam, and Christianity. But the impact of the Crusades was felt throughout that region of the world and in Europe.

The First Crusade was launched in late 1095 and ended with the capture of Jerusalem in 1099. The last Crusade took place in the late 1200s. Historians identify seven separate Crusades, although there were two other highly irregular Crusades that are not generally numbered. The exact number is not important, for the Crusades were a single extended conflict that was fought over the course of two centuries. As the military and diplomatic situation in Jerusalem and the surrounding areas changed, successive waves of European troops flowed into the region to capture a key city or to expel an opposing army that had recaptured the same city. Each of these waves represented one of the Crusades. After each Crusade, particularly the early ones, some of the European invaders remained in the Middle East to rule over Christian kingdoms they had established. Many others returned to their homelands. During the periods between each Crusade, there was relative peace between the warring parties, although tensions simmered beneath the surface.

The Muslim world was slow to respond to the Crusaders. For many decades Muslims were too busy fighting among themselves for power and influence in the Middle East and lands beyond to recognize the threat that the Crusaders posed. Only after they mounted organized resistance were they able to drive the Crusaders out of the Middle East. Hundreds of years later, many Muslims continue to regard westerners as "crusaders" bent on occupying their holy territory.

Historians continue to debate whether, from a European Christian perspective, the Crusades were a success. While the first ended successfully with the capture of Jerusalem, some of the later Crusades were military and political disasters, at least from the point of view of the Europeans. All historians agree, though, that the Crusades would have a profound effect on the development of European civilization. They opened trade routes and promoted commerce, they led to never-before-seen exploration and cultural contact, and they provided inspiration for poets and novelists. They also laid the groundwork for conflict and religious strife that continues in the twenty-first century.

Features and Format

The Crusades: Primary Sources offers twenty-four full or excerpted documents, speeches, and literary works from the Crusades era. Included are "political" statements, such as

Pope Urban II's speech calling for the First Crusade. There are also accounts of battles and sieges as well as other events, such as the Children's Crusade and the slaughter of Jews in Europe by Crusaders on their way to the Holy Land. Included are samplings from literature, among them, excerpts from the epic poem *The Song of Roland* and a chapter of the Koran. The Arabic view of the times is featured in such writings as a Muslim historian's view of the Mongol invasions. The Byzantine perspective is seen, for example, in a letter from the Eastern Orthodox patriarch of Antioch to the king of France and portions of *The Alexiad,* a biography of the emperor Alexius I Comnenus by his daughter.

The excerpts presented in *The Crusades: Primary Sources* are divided into four chapters. Each chapter focuses on a specific theme: Fighting the Holy Wars, Call to Arms, A Different View, and A Matter of Faith. Every chapter opens with an overview, followed by reprinted documents from the time of the Crusades.

The following additional material accompanies each excerpt (or section of excerpts):

- An **introduction** places the document and its author in a historical context.

- **Things to remember while reading** gives important background information and directs the reader to central ideas in the text.

- **What happened next...** gives an account of later historical events.

- **Did you know...** cites significant and interesting facts about the document, the author, or the events discussed.

- **Consider the following...** poses questions about the material for the reader to consider.

- **For More Information** lists sources for more information on the author, topic, or document.

The Crusades: Primary Sources includes numerous sidebars, highlighting interesting related information. More than forty black-and-white images illustrate the text. A glossary running alongside each primary document defines terms, people, and ideas contained in the document. The volume begins with a timeline of events and a listing of important words to know; it concludes with a subject index of people, places, and events.

The Crusades Reference Library

The Crusades: Primary Sources is only one component of a three-part U•X•L Crusades Reference Library. The set also includes one almanac volume and one volume of biographies:

- *The Crusades: Almanac* covers the Crusades in thirteen thematic chapters, each examining an element of the two-hundred-year time period. The volume takes the reader through many aspects of this lengthy conflict. Included are chapters on the origins, history, and aftermath of the Crusades and on the holy city of Jerusalem and the land of Palestine as the focal site of three faiths. There are also profiles of the various groups of Muslims and Christians involved in the fight and descriptions of knights and the conduct of warfare.

- *The Crusades: Biographies* presents the biographies of twenty-five men and women who lived at the time of the Crusades and experienced the battles or the effects of these wars. Profiled are famous figures, such as King Richard the Lionheart of England, the Muslim warrior Saladin, and Saint Francis of Assisi. Among the lesser-known people featured are the sultana of Egypt Shajarat al-Durr and the Arab soldier and writer Usamah ibn Munqidh.

Acknowledgments

Several people deserve our gratitude for their assistance with this project. We are indebted to everyone at U•X•L and Thomson Gale who assisted with the production, particularly Julie Carnagie, who provided help at all stages; we also thank Carol Nagel for her support.

Marcia Merryman Means
Neil Schlager

About the Author

J. Sydney Jones is the author of eight books of fiction and nonfiction, all with a focus on history and travel. A former journalist, he has also penned more than a thousand articles for newspapers, magazines, and biographical reference works. His works have been translated into French, Russian, Italian, German, and Hebrew.

About the Editors

Marcia Merryman Means and Neil Schlager are managing editor and president, respectively, of Schlager Group Inc., an editorial services company with offices in Florida and Vermont. Schlager Group publications have won numerous honors, including four RUSA awards from the American Library Association, two Reference Books Bulletin/Booklist Editors' Choice awards, two New York Public Library Outstanding Reference awards, and two *CHOICE* awards.

Comments and Suggestions

We welcome your comments on *The Crusades: Primary Sources* and suggestions for other topics in history to consider. Please write to Editors, *The Crusades: Primary Sources,* U•X•L, 27500 Drake Road, Farmington Hills, Michigan 48331-3535; call toll-free 800-877-4253; send faxes to 248-699-8097; or send e-mail via http://www.galegroup.com.

Timeline of Events

Seventh Century A great victory is celebrated in an excerpt from the **Koran,** the holy book of the Muslims.

c. 1000 In **"The Prior Who Became a Moslem,"** a tale from *The Arabian Nights,* readers can see the power of faith and religion in the Middle East at the time of the Crusades.

November 28, 1095 Pope Urban II calls for a holy war, or Crusade, against the Muslims in the Holy Land and Constantinople in a **"Speech at the Council of Clermont."**

May 27, 1096 The twelfth-century Jewish chronicler Soloman bar Samson describes the persecution of the Jews at the time of the First Crusade in **"The Crusaders in Mainz."**

1097 Anna Comnena, princess of the Byzantine Empire, writes of the arrival of the Crusaders in Constantinople and their early victories in excerpts from *The Alexiad.*

March 29, 1098 Stephen of Blois, one of the leaders of the First Crusade, writes **"To His Wife Adele"** at the time of the siege of Antioch.

c. 1100 *The Song of Roland,* a long French poem, provides insight into the European views about Muslims at the beginning of the Crusades.

Early twelfth century The Muslim poet Abu al-Musaffar al-Abiwardi provides the shocked view of Islam on the capture of Jerusalem by the Crusaders in "**Poem on the Crusades.**"

1107 The Russian churchman Abbot Daniel describes a miracle in Jerusalem with "**The Holy Light; How It Descends upon the Holy Sepulchre.**"

1120 The Persian poet and mathematician Omar Khayyam explains his personal religion in "**Profession of Faith.**"

1128 The French religious thinker Bernard of Clairvaux writes in favor of the Knights Templars with "**In Praise of the New Knighthood.**"

1147 A "**Hostile View of the Crusades**" is provided in an excerpt from the *Annales Herbipolenses.*

1164 The Eastern Orthodox Church leader Aymeric warns the king of France of "**The Decline of Christian Power in the Holy Land.**"

1188 England's King Henry II establishes "**The Saladin Tithe**" to help finance the Third Crusade.

Late twelfth century The Muslim view of the Crusaders, or Franks, is provided by the nobleman Usamah ibn Munqidh in excerpts from his memoir, *An Arab-Syrian Gentleman and Warrior in the Period of the Crusades.*

Late twelfth century The Spanish Jewish scholar and traveler Benjamin of Tudela provides insights into the Jewish situation at the time of the Crusades in *The Itinerary of Benjamin Tudela.*

Thirteenth century The Muslim historian Ibn Said describes in *Book of the Maghrib* how fragmented the Islamic world was at the time of the Crusades. Because of competing dynasties and religious groups, the Muslims were at first unable to unite and fight the Christians.

1207   The Crusader Geoffrey de Villehardouin gives a first-hand account of the Fourth Crusade in excerpts from ***Chronicle of the Fourth Crusade and the Conquest of Constantinople.***

1212   An account of The Children's Crusade from ***Chronica Regiae Coloniensis*** reminds readers of the unintended consequences of Crusader enthusiasm.

1219   The French poet Conon de Béthune promotes the Cusades in **"Ahi! Amours! Com dure departie / Alas, Love, What Hard Leave."**

1220–21 The historian Ibn al-Athir provides a chilling description of the cruelty of the invading Mongols in **"On the Tatars."**

1229   The emperor of the Holy Roman Empire writes to the king of England to praise his own peace treaty with the sultan al-Kamil, which won back Jerusalem for the Christians in **"Frederick II to Henry III of England."**

1229   The patriarch of Jerusalem complains about Frederick's peace treaty with al-Kamil in **"Gerold to All the Faithful,"** from *Chronica Majora.*

1244   The master, or leader, of the Knights Hospitallers describes the complex system of alliances, or partnerships, in the Holy Land and how the Turks took back the Holy City in **"The Capture of Jerusalem, 1244"** from the *Chronica Majora.*

1265   A sample of medieval anti-Semitic laws is given in **"*Las Siete Partidas:* Laws on Jews."**

1291   Ludolph of Suchem describes the final curtain in the Crusades with **"The Fall of Acre, 1291."**

Words to Know

A

Abbasid: A Muslim religious dynasty that could trace its origins back to the uncle of Muhammad, the prophet and founder of Islam. The Abbasids ruled in Baghdad from 749 to 1258 and were the spiritual heart of Sunni Islam, the orthodox, or mainstream, branch of the faith.

Abbey: Society of monks or nuns governed by an abbot or an abbess, respectively; also refers to the buildings in which these monks and nuns resided.

Allah: The name of the Muslim god.

Asia Minor: The peninsula between the Mediterranean Sea and the Black Sea that holds most of present-day Turkey; also sometimes referred to as Anatolia.

Assassins: An extremist group of Muslim Shiites organized in the late eleventh century to fight their opponents by any means possible. Known to fortify themselves for their work using *hashishin,* or the drug hashish, they came to be known in French as "assassins," and the name later came to be used to describe those who plotted murder, especially for political reasons.

Atabeg: A Turkish title meaning "prince-father," given to a local leader or governor.

B

Babylon: An ancient city in Mesopotamia, modern-day Iraq, and also the European name for Cairo, Egypt, at the time of the Crusades.

Basileus: The official title of the emperors of the Byzantine Empire.

Bishop: A high rank or office in the medieval church. A person holding this office usually presided over a territory called a diocese, or see.

Brethren: Fellow members of a religious order or group.

Bull: An official Catholic Church declaration or document; sometimes referred to as a papal ("from the pope") bull.

Byzantine Empire: The Eastern Roman Empire, established in the fourth century in Constantinople and comprising present-day Greece, Turkey, and part of the Balkan countries.

C

Caliph: The English adaptation of the Arab word *khalifa,* which means "successor." This was a title adapted by early Muslim leaders after the death in 632 of Muhammad, the founder of Islam. Rulers in name only by the time of the Crusades, the caliphs were still important religious leaders for the Islamic world. The region a caliph controlled was called a caliphate.

Castle: Defensive residence of a lord or prince.

Cavalry: A military body that uses horses in battle.

Chansons de geste: Epic poems of medieval France written between the eleventh and thirteenth centuries. *The Song of Roland* is an example of such a long poem about heroic deeds.

Clergy: Those authorized by the church to hold religious services.

Constantinople: Capital of the Byzantine Empire, founded by Emperor Constantine in the fourth century; present-day Istanbul, in Turkey

Courtly love: Pure love of a knight for a fair damsel, a pretty and chaste, or virgin, woman.

Crown: The circlet, usually of gold or silver, worn on the head of the king or emperor to show his office. It also means the power of the king or the kingdom.

Crusades: The holy wars fought between Christians and Muslims over occupancy of the shrines of the Holy Land. Begun in 1096, these wars ended with the fall of Acre in 1291 and the final defeat of the Christian armies in the Middle East. Depending on the history consulted, there were seven or eight major Crusades.

D

Diplomacy: The practice of conducting international relations, such as making treaties and alliances.

Dome of the Rock: A shrine in Jerusalem important to both Muslims and those of the Jewish faith.

Duke: Highest level of the nobility, ranking just below prince.

Dynasty: A line of rulers that come from the same family or group.

E

Emir: A Turkish title that indicates a military leader or commander, used widely throughout the Muslim world at the time of the Crusades.

Empire: A political unit consisting of several territories governed by a single supreme authority, usually called the emperor.

Excommunicate: To expel a person from the Catholic Church.

F

Fast: To refrain from eating for religious purposes.

Fatimid: The ruling dynasty of Egypt from 969 to 1167. A Shiite dynasty, it based its claim to power on its connection to Fatima, the daughter of the prophet Muhammad.

Frank: The Muslim word for Crusader, because many of them were Frankish, or French; also sometimes called Franj.

H

Holy Land: For Christians of the West this means Jerusalem and the sites in Palestine identified with the birth and early life of Jesus Christ.

Holy Roman Empire: A loose collection of German and Italian principalities and territories that lasted from the tenth to the nineteenth century.

I

Islam: The religious faith of the Muslims, which is based on the words and teaching of the prophet Muhammad.

J

Jihad: Holy war of the Muslims against unbelievers in their faith.

Jongleur: Medieval entertainers; those who performed the troubadour poems and songs.

K

King: Crowned ruler of a territory or country called a kingdom. The term comes from the German word *koennen,* meaning "to be able."

Knight: A feudal tenant, usually a member of the nobility, who served his superior, or lord, as a mounted soldier.

Knights Hospitallers: Religious military order established in 1113 to help sick pilgrims in the Holy Land.

Knights Templars: Religious military order established in 1118 to defend Christian pilgrims in the Holy Land.

Koran: See **Qur'an.**

L

Lord: In feudal society, the owner of a manor, or great house, and lands granted directly by the king. The lord, in turn, gave land to the vassals who served him.

M

Madrassa: College for study of the Qur'an.

Mamluk: From the Arab verb for "to own," meaning a slave. In Muslim societies they were usually Turkish slaves trained to be soldiers and commanders. Also refers to the dynasty ruling Egypt from 1252 to 1517.

Mercenary: Soldier for hire.

Middle Ages: The historical period from approximately 500 to 1500 C.E. As an adjective, "medieval" often is used to refer to this era.

Middle East: A term used in the West to indicate the regions that include the present-day countries of Cyprus, the Asian part of Turkey, Syria, Lebanon, Israel, the West Bank and Gaza, Jordan, Iraq, Iran, the countries of the Arabian peninsula (Saudi Arabia, Yemen, Oman, United Arab Emirates, Qatar, Bahrain, and Kuwait), Egypt, and Libya. Also used to describe the lands of the region that have an Islamic culture.

Minnesänger (MINN-uh-seng-er): A medieval German knight, poet, and singer of courtly love.

Mongols: A nomadic, warlike tribe from the steppes of Central Asia that, under the leadership of Genghis Khan and his offspring, invaded the Middle East and Europe during the thirteenth century; also called Tatars or Tartars.

Monk: Member of a religious order, or group, that stays out of society and honors hard work, silence, and devotion to God and prayer.

Moors: Muslims from North Africa who settled in Spain in the Middle Ages.

Mosque: Islamic place of worship.

Muslim: Follower of the Islamic faith; also called Moslem.

N

Nobility: As a group, members of a noble, or aristocratic, family.

O

Outremer (oo-tre-MARE): The name for the Crusader kingdoms and states in the Holy Land. From the Latin, the word means "beyond the sea."

P

Palestine: In the Middle Ages, the region thought of as the Holy Land on the east coast of the Mediterranean Sea. It was made up of present-day Jordan, Israel, and parts of Egypt.

Papacy: The church office of the pope.

Patriarch: Major leaders of the Eastern Orthodox, or Greek Orthodox, Church, similar in power to bishops of the Catholic Church. The four major patriarchs in the East were in Jerusalem, Antioch, Constantinople, and Alexandria.

Pilgrimage: A journey made to a sacred place for religious purposes. A person who takes such a journey is called a pilgrim.

Pope: Leader of the Roman Catholic Church; in the Middle Ages, the religious leader of the Christian West.

Prelate: A high church officer.

Prince: A ruler, from the Latin *princeps,* meaning "first in rank." In general, any ruler came to be known as the prince. A male heir in a royal household, the "crown" prince, was the first in line to the throne, or kingship.

Principality: A subdivision of a kingdom.

Propaganda: Information, often false, that is widely spread in order to help or harm a nation or a cause.

Q

Qur'an: The Muslim holy book, also known as the Koran.

R

Rabbi: A religious leader and scholar in the Jewish faith.

Ransom: The money paid to free a knight or other noble person captured in battle.

Reign: The length of rule of a king, emperor, or other noble.

Remission of sins: Forgiveness of sins; during the time of the Crusades, of those who volunteered to go on Crusade.

S

Saracen: A member of the nomadic people of the Syrian and Arabian deserts at the time of the Roman Empire; more generally applied by Europeans to all Arabs and Muslims during the Crusades.

Seljuk Turks: A Turkish tribe from Central Asia that converted to Islam and invaded the Middle East in the eleventh century. Religious fanatics, they threatened access to the holy sites of Christianity in Palestine.

Sharia: The religious law of Islam.

Shiite: A follower of the Islamic branch founded by the fourth caliph, Ali, cousin and son-in-law to Muhammad; the first important minority branch of Islam.

Siege: Military blockade of a city or fort to make it surrender.

Sufi: A Muslim mystic.

Sunni: The majority branch of Islam, taking their authority not from direct descendants of Muhammad but from the *sunna,* or practices of Muhammad.

T

Talmud: The body of Jewish laws included in books called the Mishnah and the Gemara.

Tatars: See **Mongols.**

Teutonic Knights: A religious and military order of knights restricted to German membership, which split off from the Knights Hospitallers.

Tithe: A religious tax or offering, often 10 percent of a person's annual income.

Torah: The first five books of the Old Testament, which form part of the Jewish tradition of literature and religious laws.

Troubadour: A noble poet and writer of songs in the south of France at the time of the Crusades.

Trouvèes: Troubadours of northern France.

U

Umayyad: An early Muslim dynasty that lost its power in the Middle East and took refuge in Cordova, Spain. There, it established a Spanish Islamic dynasty lasting from 1056 to 1269, noted for an emphasis on scholarship and religious diversity.

Z

Zangid: Muslim dynasty of Turkish origin founded by the military leader Zengi in 1127. It ruled in Syria and northern Iraq until 1222 and was based in the cities of Mosul, Aleppo, and Damascus.

Fighting the Holy Wars

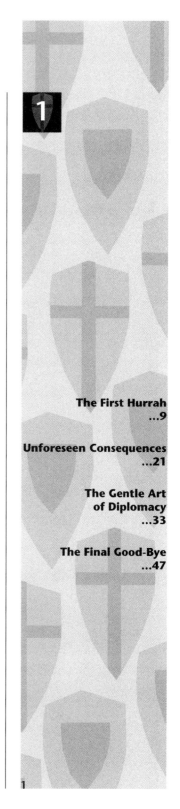

1

The Crusades began in 1095 and raged, on and off, for the next two hundred years. During these centuries, the western Christian world pitted itself against what it thought of as the infidel, or the unbelievers, in the Middle East. In particular, Crusaders, (those who had "taken the cross," as this fighting for Christianity was called at the time), were battling for reoccupation of the shrines and sites holy to Christians in Palestine: Jerusalem, Nazareth, and Bethlehem. These locations along a narrow strip of the eastern coast of the Mediterranean Sea, sacred not only to Christians but also to Jews and members of the Islamic faith, had been contested for centuries. Although Muslims (believers in Islam and the words of the prophet Muhammad) had occupied Jerusalem since the seventh century, they had generally recognized the rights of those of other religions to have free access to the city. Thus Muslims, Christians, and Jews had lived in relative harmony in Jerusalem. A wrinkle was thrown into this balancing act in the eleventh century with the arrival of a new power in the Middle East: the Seljuk Turks.

This nomadic, warrior-like tribe of Turks from Central Asia had made its way into Anatolia and Asia Minor by the eleventh century, converted to Islam, and become fanatical, or extremist, defenders of that religion. Where before there was compromise between the Christian and Muslim inhabitants of the region, now, with the sudden power swing toward the Seljuks, intolerance was on the rise. The Seljuk Turks threatened the Byzantine Empire (Eastern Roman Empire) in Asia Minor, defeating the emperor's troops at the Battle of Manzikert in 1071. Invited into one of the major centers of Islamic civilization, Baghdad, as "protectors" of the faith, the Seljuks proceeded to sweep west and south through Syria and into Palestine, ultimately occupying Jerusalem itself in 1071. No longer were Christians allowed to visit the sites found there that were connected with the birth and early life of Jesus Christ; even the Holy Sepulchre, the tomb of Christ, was off limits to Christian pilgrims, or religious visitors.

These events did not go unnoticed in the West. As early as 1094 or 1095 the *basileus,* (emperor of the Byzantine Empire) Alexius I Comnenus, wrote to Pope Urban II, the head of the Christian church in Europe, asking for help against the Turks. Urban II took this cry for assistance to heart for several reasons. For Urban II it was important on religious grounds that Christians have access to the sites in the Holy Land, a region then known as Palestine. He also wanted to restore good relations between the two branches of Christianity: the Roman Catholic Church based in Europe, and the Eastern Orthodox Church in Constantinople, capital of the Byzantine Empire. These two branches had been quarreling for centuries and had lately come to new lows in their relations. Another consideration for Urban II was the situation in Europe itself, a continent torn apart by small wars between minor nobles and professional soldiers (knights) who had, it seemed, too much time on their hands. Many of these nobles had older brothers who were going to inherit the lands of their fathers, leaving the younger siblings without resources. In other words, Europe was full of underemployed soldiers eager for a fight and for new opportunities. Urban II wanted to ship these aggressive knights abroad and use their skills to fight for Christianity. These knights would then carve out Crusader kingdoms for themselves in the Holy Land.

In 1095, at the religious conference called the Council of Clermont, Pope Urban II called for a holy war, a Crusade (from the Latin word for "cross") to liberate the Holy Land from the Muslims. He spoke of harsh treatment of Christians at the hands of the Muslims. Whether or not such tales were true, they did convince those gathered to hear the pope that such a war was necessary. At the end of his passionate speech, the nobles in the audience shouted out, "*Deus volt!*," Latin for "God wills it." This became the battle cry of Crusaders in the Holy Land.

Although the primary motivation for the Crusades was religious, there were other factors involved. Historian Karen Armstrong noted the variety of motivations in her Crusades history, *Holy War:*

> The Crusades, like so much of the modern conflict, were not wholly rational movements that could be explained away by purely economic or territorial ambition or by the clash of rights and interests. They were fueled, on all sides, by myths and passions that were far more effective in getting people to act than any purely political motivation. The medieval holy wars in the Middle East could not be solved by rational treatises [discussions] or neat territorial solutions. Fundamental [basic] passions were involved which touched the identity of Christians, Muslims and Jews and which were sacred to the identity of each. They have not changed very much in the holy wars of today.

From 1095 to the end of the thirteenth century there were seven major Crusades, perhaps more or fewer, depending on which historian is consulted. There were also numerous smaller expeditions from time to time during these two hundred years. Some were sponsored by the papacy (the office of the pope); others by kings or emperors; and still others, such as the ill-fated People's Crusade (1096) and the Children's Crusade (1212), by common people who were filled with religious enthusiasm. Though the First Crusade (1095–99) succeeded in winning back Jerusalem for the West, most Crusades ended in disaster from the Christian point of view. The First Crusade was led by nobles, such as Godfrey of Bouillon and his brother, Baldwin, along with Count Raymond of Toulouse, Count Stephen of Blois, and the Norman prince from southern Italy, Bohemund, and succeeded in capturing a strip of land along the eastern Mediterranean from Antioch in the north to

Jerusalem in the south. This conquered territory was called the Latin Kingdom, and its center was in Jerusalem for as long as that city stayed in Crusader hands. The Crusader states, consisting of the Kingdom of Jerusalem, Principality of Antioch, County of Tripoli, and County of Edessa, lasted until 1291 with the fall of the city of Acre.

During those years there was a constant struggle between the Christian Crusaders of this Latin Kingdom, or Outremer (literally "beyond the sea" in Latin), as it was called in Europe, and the Muslims who surrounded them. The Crusaders built fortresses, birthed dynasties, and founded fighting religious orders, such as the Knights Templar and Hospitallers and the Teutonic Knights, which together formed the elite corps of troops protecting Outremer from invasion. Meanwhile, the Muslims, who included ethnic Arabs, Turks, and Egyptians, occasionally produced great leaders to rally the Islamic world and overcome their own internal rivalries in order to concentrate on fighting the European invaders. The idea of *jihad*, or holy war, became a unifying principle for Islam just as it had for Christians. Under leaders such as the Turkish Zengi and his son, Nur al-Din in the early to mid-twelfth century; the great Kurdish military strategist Saladin in the late twelfth century; and the Mamluk, or slave, leaders of Egypt Baybars and Kalavun in the thirteenth century, the Muslims managed to push the Crusaders into an ever-smaller pocket next to the Mediterranean until finally driving the Europeans out of the Middle East in 1291.

The West sent inspired leaders as well. Eleanor of Aquitaine and her husband, Louis VII of France, followed the call of Saint Bernard of Clairvaux to fight, unsuccessfully, the rising power of Islam during the Second Crusade (1147–49). Similarly, Richard the Lionheart of England and Philip Augustus of France fought in the Third Crusade (1189–91) after Saladin recaptured Jerusalem for Islam. The Fourth Crusade (1202–04) was perhaps one of the most disastrous from a western point of view, for the Crusaders never reached the Holy Land. Instead, they were drawn into rivalries over the succession to the throne of the Byzantine Empire and destroyed Constantinople in 1204. This resulted in the establishment of a Latin Kingdom in Asia Minor that lasted for more than half a century and further worsened relationships between the eastern and western churches. Egypt was the center of the Fifth

A papal legate returning the cross to King Louis IX right before the beginning of the Seventh and final Crusade. *Musee Conde, Chantilly, France/Bridgeman Art Library. Reproduced by permission.*

Crusade (1218–21), and once again the Christian forces were unsuccessful in dislodging the Muslims from Jerusalem. This was accomplished, for a time, by the peaceful means of diplomacy (international relations) between Frederick II, the emperor of the Holy Roman Empire (known also as the German Kingdom) and the sultan, or ruler, of Egypt, al-Malik al-Kamil. Yet only fifteen years later the Turkish Muslims once again seized Jerusalem, setting off the Seventh Crusade (1248–54), led by France's Louis IX. Once more the Crusaders tried to reach Jerusalem via Egypt, and once more they were defeated by the sultan's forces. Louis IX was captured and forced to pay a heavy price for his release. Some historians acknowledge an Eighth Crusade (1270), when Louis IX once again took up the cross and tried for a back-door entrance to Jerusalem via the North African desert, where he, his son, and thousands of Crusaders died of fever, ending the Crusade before it had really begun.

The Crusades changed the world in major ways, both good and bad. On the plus side, there was a meeting of cultures in the Middle East. Christian knights and Crusaders brought back Arab scholarship, customs, and artistic influences, thus putting Europe in touch with a rich cultural tradition. This cultural contact, in turn, helped bring about the flowering of European culture during the Renaissance of the fourteenth and fifteenth centuries. Commerce also increased between these two parts of the world, leading to increased standards of living on both sides. Additionally, the power of kings and secular (nonreligious) leaders grew during this period, while the power of the church and the pope declined. This was a direct result of the fact that such secular leaders were in charge of the crusading enterprises, even though the pope many times had called for them to be organized. This new balance of power between church and state eventually led to the modern nation-state. On the downside, the idea of international war against the enemies of Christianity or the established church became a part of European thinking. This attitude fueled wars during the Protestant Reformation of the sixteenth century. Worst of all, relations between Christians and Muslims were poisoned for centuries, a consequence the modern world is still living with.

The great events of these Crusades—the battles, treaties, and infighting—were recorded by historians, clergy, and fighting men and women on all sides. In the beginning section of this chapter, "The First Hurrah," the focus is the First Crusade, perhaps the only successful such mission to the Holy Land. Portions of *The Alexiad,* a biography of Byzantine Emperor Alexius I written by his daughter Anna, and a Crusader letter written by one of the leaders of the First Crusade, from *Translations and Reprints from the Original Sources of European History,* provide the human side of this holy war from the perspectives of the Byzantines and of the invading Christians. The second section, "Unforeseen Consequences," offers two instances of tragic results of the Crusades, with excerpts from *Chronicles of the Fourth Crusade and the Conquest of Constantinople,* written by a French participant in that Crusade, and from *The Crusades: A Documentary History.* The third section, "The Gentle Art of Diplomacy," offers two interpretations of the treaty won by Frederick II during the Sixth Crusade, with excerpts from *Translations and Reprints from the Original Sources of European History* and from the *Internet Medieval Sourcebook.* The last section of this chapter, "The Final

Good-Bye," tells two episodes in the final act of the Crusaders in the Middle East: the taking of Jerusalem by Turkish Muslim warriors in 1244, described in a letter from the leader of the Knights Hospitallers who fought there, and the fall of Acre in 1291, with an excerpt from the *Description of the Holy Land and of the Way Thither* by a fourteenth-century visitor to Jerusalem, Ludolph of Suchem.

The First Hurrah

Excerpt "Stephen, Count of Blois and Chartres, To His Wife Adele" (1098)

Originally written by Stephen of Blois; Reprinted in "Letters of the Crusades," from *Translations and Reprints from the Original Sources of European History*; Edited by Dana Munro; Published in 1896

Excerpt from The Alexiad *(c. 1148)*

Originally written by Anna Comnena; Translated by Elizabeth A. Dawes; Published in 1928

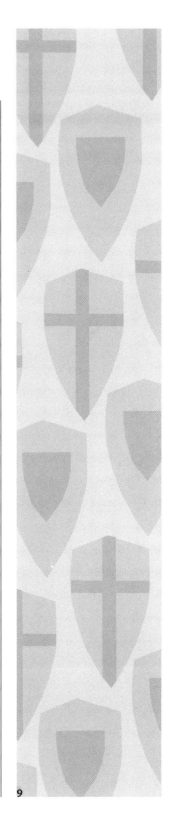

The Council of Clermont was called by Pope Urban II in November of 1095. Various pieces of church business were dealt with over the several days of the conference, but on the final day the pope called for a holy war to overthrow the Muslims from power in the Holy Land and return it to Christian domination. Urban II played up the desperate situation of the Byzantine Empire and also the supposed mistreatment of Christians at the hands of Muslims in the region. His words were met with excited approval, and as a result, the First Crusade was officially launched. It would take more than half a year, however, to organize the mission. Western leaders slowly began gathering their soldiers while the wandering preacher Peter the Hermit roused the people of Europe with his fiery speeches and sermons. The people he thus inflamed with the Crusader cause grew impatient. They did not want to wait for the nobility to collect their armies; instead, they formed what became known as the "People's Crusade," an army of poor farmers and laborers who set out—men, women, and children—in the spring of 1096 for Constantinople, where the Crusade was to begin. Led by

Peter the Hermit and Walter the Penniless, these followers were poorly equipped and attempted to live off the land as they crossed Europe and headed southwest for Constantinople. In Hungary and Bulgaria they caused great unrest, and thousands among these unlikely Crusaders and the local populations died in disputes over food and property.

The Byzantines were shocked when this mob arrived. They had been expecting an elite corps of soldiers to help them battle the Seljuk Turks, and now they were stuck with this undisciplined crowd. The Byzantine emperor was happy to ferry them across the narrow straits and into Asia Minor, where they were promptly destroyed by the Turks in August 1096. At about this same time, the real Crusader armies began arriving in Constantinople. These Crusaders included Godfrey of Bouillon, who later became the unofficial leader; Raymond of Toulouse, the oldest and best-known of the nobles; Robert of Flanders; Stephen of Blois; and Bohemund of Sicily, who arrived only in April 1097. No kings took part in the First Crusade, and most of the armies were led by French-speaking knights. For this reason, the soldiers quickly became known to the Byzantines and the Muslims as Franks.

Again the Byzantine emperor, Alexius I, was surprised by the force sent to help him. These knights seemed to have their own plans. Although he attempted to have them pledge their loyalty to him, it quickly became clear that the Crusaders were not simply on a goodwill mission. Relations were never very good between the Byzantines and the Crusaders. The first major battle of the Crusade, at the city of Nicaea, close to Constantinople, made it apparent to both sides that they could not trust each other. As the Crusaders were busy attacking the gates, Alexius I plotted behind the scenes to work out a handover of the city from the Turks. By the time the Crusaders entered, the Byzantine flag was already flying over the city.

The victory at Dorylaeum on July 1, 1097, proved to be more of a cooperative effort, however. The Turks attacked the advancing Crusader army, but the Christians held their ground and were aided by the Byzantines, driving the Muslims off. The Crusader army pushed on across Anatolia and south to the great city of Antioch, arriving on October 20, 1097. There they found a well-fortified city that would not be easily captured. The Crusaders gathered their forces for a long and difficult siege. A letter from Stephen of Blois to his wife and excerpts from Anna Comnena's *The Alexiad* provide different viewpoints of this first major conflict of the First Crusade. Stephen of Blois was one of the nobles who participated in the siege of Antioch, and his description of events to his wife adds a more personal glimpse into the costs of war. Anna Comnena, daughter of the Byzantine emperor, wrote the biographical account of her father's deeds late in life, relying on memory and court records.

Anna Comnena who wrote *The Alexiad,* the biographical account of her father, Byzantine emperor Alexius I. *Photograph courtesy of The Library of Congress.*

Things to Remember While Reading Excerpts on the taking of Antioch:

- The Crusader army that gathered at Constantinople numbered about four thousand mounted (horse-riding) knights and at least twenty-five thousand foot soldiers. Simply feeding such an army was a difficult task.

- Antioch was the third great city of the old Roman Empire. At the time of the First Crusade, it was strongly fortified with more than four hundred towers built along its huge walls.

- The siege of Antioch lasted seven and a half months, from October 20, 1097, to June 3, 1098. Then the Crusaders themselves, having taken the city, were put under siege for another three weeks by a Muslim army.

Excerpt: "Stephen, Count of Blois and Chartres, To His Wife Adele"

*Count Stephen to Adele, his sweetest and most amiable wife, to his dear children, and to all his **vassals** of all ranks—his greeting and blessing.*

*You may be very sure, dearest, that the messenger whom I sent to give you pleasure, left me before Antioch safe and unharmed and through God's grace in the greatest prosperity. And already at that time, together with all the chosen army of Christ, endowed with great **valor** by Him, we had been continuously advancing for twenty-three weeks toward the home of our Lord Jesus. You may know for certain, my beloved, that of gold, silver and many other kind of riches I now have twice as much as your love had assigned to me when I left you. For all our princes, with the common consent of the whole army, against my own wishes, have made me up to the present time the leader, chief and director of their whole expedition.*

*You have certainly heard that after the capture of the city of Nicaea we fought a great battle with the **perfidious** Turks and by God's aid conquered them. Next we conquered for the Lord all Romania and afterwards Cappadocia. And we learned that there was a certain Turkish prince Assam, dwelling in Cappadocia; **thither** we directed our course. All his castles we conquered by force and compelled him to flee to a certain very strong castle situated on a high rock. We also gave the land of that Assam to one of our chiefs and in order that he might conquer the above-mentioned Assam, we left there with him many **soldiers of Christ**. **Thence**, continually following the wicked Turks, we drove them through the midst of Armenia, as far as the great river Euphrates. Having left all their baggage and beasts of burden on the bank, they fled across the river into Arabia.*

*The bolder of the Turkish soldiers, indeed, entering Syria, hastened by forced marches night and day, in order to be able to enter the royal city of Antioch before our approach. The whole army of God learning this gave due praise and thanks to the **omnipotent** Lord. Hastening with great joy to the aforesaid chief city of Antioch, we besieged it and very often had many conflicts there with the Turks; and seven times with the citizens of Antioch and with the **innumerable** troops coming to its aid, whom we rushed to meet, we*

Vassals: Subordinates or underlings.

Valor: Courage, bravery.

Perfidious: Untrustworthy.

Thither: In that direction.

Soldiers of Christ: Crusaders.

Thence: From there.

Omnipotent: All-powerful.

Innumerable: Countless, numerous.

The Crusades: Primary Sources

fought with the fiercest courage, under the leadership of Christ. And in all these seven battles, by the aid of the Lord God, we conquered and most assuredly killed an innumerable host of them. In those battles, indeed, and in very many attacks made upon the city, many of our **brethren** and followers were killed and their souls were borne to the joys of paradise.

We found the city of Antioch very extensive, fortified with incredible strength and almost **impregnable**. In addition, more than 5,000 bold Turkish soldiers had entered the city, not counting the Saracens, Publicans, Arabs, Turcopolitans, Syrians, Armenians and other different races of whom an infinite **multitude** had gathered together there. In fighting against these enemies of God and of our own we have, by God's grace, endured many sufferings and innumerable evils up to the present time. Many also have already exhausted all their resources in this very holy passion. Very many of our Franks, indeed, would have met a **temporal** death from starvation, if the **clemency** of God and our money had not **succoured** them. Before the above-mentioned city of Antioch indeed, throughout the whole winter we suffered for our Lord Christ from excessive cold and enormous torrents of rain. What some say about the impossibility of bearing the heat of the sun throughout Syria is untrue, for the winter there is very similar to our winter in the West.

When truly Caspian [Bagi Seian], the emir of Antioch—that is, prince and lord—perceived that he was hard pressed by us, he sent his son Sensodolo [Chems Eddaulab] by name, to the prince who holds Jerusalem, and to the prince of Calep, Rodoarn [Rodoanus], and to Docap [Deccacus Ibn Toutousch], prince of Damascus. He also sent into Arabia to Bolianuth and to Carathania to Hamelnuth. These five **emirs** with 12,000 picked Turkish horsemen suddenly came to aid the inhabitants of Antioch. We, indeed, ignorant of all this, had sent many of our soldiers away to the cities and fortresses. For there are one hundred and sixty-five cities and fortresses throughout Syria which are in our power. But a little before they reached the city, we attacked them at three **leagues**' distance with 700 soldiers, on a certain plain near the "Iron Bridge." God, however, fought for us, His faithful, against them. For on that day, fighting in the strength that God gives, we conquered them and killed an innumerable multitude—God continually fighting for us—and we also carried back to the army more than two hundred of their heads, in order that the people might rejoice on that account. The emperor of Babylon also sent Saracen messengers to our army with letters, and through these he established peace and concord with us.

Brethren: Brothers, comrades.

Impregnable: Unable to be penetrated or destroyed.

Multitude: Crowd, throng.

Temporal: Worldly.

Clemency: Mercy.

Succoured: Assisted.

Emirs: A Middle-Eastern prince or chieftain.

League: A measure of distance, approximately three miles.

Crusaders using a catapult to siege the city of Antioch during the First Crusade as described by Stephen, the count of Blois. © *Leonard de Selva/Corbis. Reproduced by permission.*

Lent: A time of fasting and penitence observed by Christians during the forty weekdays before Easter.

Mariners: Seamen.

I love to tell you, dearest, what happened to us during **Lent**. *Our princes had caused a fortress to be built which was between our camp and the sea. For the Turks daily issuing from this gate killed some of our men on their way to the sea. The city of Antioch is about five leagues' distance from the sea. For this reason they sent the excellent Bohemond and Raymond, count of St. Gilles, to the sea with only sixty horsemen, in order that they might bring* **mariners** *to aid in this work. When, however, they were returning to us with those*

mariners, the Turks collected an army, fell suddenly upon our two leaders and forced them to a perilous flight. In that unexpected flight we lost more than 500 of our foot soldiers to the glory of God. Of our horsemen, however, we lost only two, for certain.

Excerpt from The Alexiad

What happened next? The **Latins** in company with the **Roman** army reached Antioch ... and paid no attention to the country on either side but drew their lines close to the walls ... and proceeded to besiege this city during three revolutions of the moon. The Turks ... sent word to the Sultan of Chorosan begging him to send sufficient troops to their assistance, in order to **succour** the Antiochians themselves, and also to drive off the Latins who were besieging them from outside.

Now there happened to be an Armenian on the tower above guarding the portion of the wall assigned to Bohemund. As he often

The conquest of Antioch by the Crusaders, as described by Anna Comnena in *The Alexiad.* © *Archivo Iconografico, S.A./Corbis. Reproduced by permission.*

Latins: Crusaders.

Roman: The Byzantines, though mostly of Greek origin, called themselves Roman, after the old Roman Empire.

Succour: Assist.

bent over from above Bohemund **plied** him with **honeyed** words, tempted him with many promises and thus persuaded him to betray the city to him. The Armenian said to him, "Whenever you like and as soon as you give me a signal from outside, I will at once hand over this tower to you. Only be quite ready yourself and have all the people with you ready too and equipped with ladders…. The whole army must be under arms so that directly the Turks see you after you have come up and hear your war-cry, they will be terrified and turn in flight." And this arrangement Bohemund kept secret. While these matters were in contemplation, a messenger came saying that an immense crowd of Hagarenes … was close at hand, under the conduct of the man called Curpagan…. When he heard this, as he did not wish to **cede** Antioch to Taticius [a Byzantine general] according to the oath he had previously sworn to the Emperor, … Bohemund planned a wicked plan which would force Taticius to remove himself from the city against his will. Accordingly he went to him and said, "I want to reveal a secret to you, as I am concerned for your safety. A report which has reached the ears of the Counts has much disturbed their minds—it is that the Emperor has persuaded the Sultan to send these men from Chorosan against us. As the Counts firmly believe this, they are plotting against your life. And now I have done my duty by warning you beforehand of the danger that threatens you. And the rest is your concern, to take measures for your own safety, and that of the troops under you." Then considering the severe famine … and also because he despaired of taking Antioch, Taticius departed, embarked on the Roman fleet which was in the harbour of Sudi, and made for Cyprus. After his departure Bohemund, who still kept the Armenian's promise secret, and was **buoyed** up by the great hope of gaining possession of Antioch for himself, said to the Counts, "You see how long we have already persevered in this siege, and yet have accomplished nothing useful … and now we are within an ace of perishing by starvation unless we can devise something better for our salvation…. God does not always give victory to the leaders by means of the sword, nor are such things always accomplished by fighting. But what toil has not **procured**, words have often **effected**, and the greatest trophies have been erected by friendly and **propitiatory intercourse**. Let us therefore … **endeavour** to accomplish something sensible and courageous for our own safety before Curpagan arrives. Let each one of us studiously try to win over the barbarian who guards our respective section. And … let there be set as prize for the one who first succeeds in this work, the sovereignty of this

Plied: Made repeated observations or requests.

Honeyed: Coaxed or flattered

Cede: Give up, surrender.

Buoyed: Cheered.

Effected: Made to happen, achieved.

Propitiatory Intercourse: Friendly discussion.

Endeavour: To try to do something.

city until such time as the man who is to take it over from us arrives from the Emperor ..." All these things that artful and ambitious Bohemund did, not so much for the sake of the Latins, and the **common weal**, as for his own advancement, and by this planning and speaking and deceiving he did not fail to gain his object.... All the Counts agreed to his proposition and set to work. And at dawn of day Bohemund at once made for the tower, and the Armenian according to agreement opened the gate to him; he immediately rushed up with his followers more quickly than can be told and was seen by the people within and without standing on the battlements of the tower and ordering the trumpeters to sound the call to battle.

And then indeed a strange sight was to be seen, the Turks, panic-stricken fled without delay through the opposite gate, and the only ones of them who stayed behind were a few brave men who defended the Cula [the citadel]; and the Franks from outside ascended the ladders on the heels of Bohemund, and straightway took possession of the city of Antioch. Tancred with a small body of men pursued the fugitives, many of whom were killed and many wounded.

What happened next...

The siege of Antioch was an up-and-down battle for the Crusaders. The Christians surrounded the fortified city all winter long, surviving cold and hunger. By January some of the Christians were already running away; among them was the Byzantine general Taticius,

Bohemund I

The Bohemund (sometimes referred to as Bohemond) of this excerpt was a fair-haired, handsome knight. Some historians have thought that perhaps Anna Comnena was in love with this swashbuckling Crusader, for she gives him many pages of her biography. A Norman with Viking blood in him, Bohemund was one of the major leaders of the First Crusade. He was the oldest son of Robert of Guiscard, something of a robber noble who stole an empire for himself and his family in southern Italy and Sicily. Bohemund and his father were no strangers to the Byzantine Empire, for they had long been at work trying to invade it and win more territory. Although he was considered an enemy of the Byzantine Empire, Bohemund actually pledged his loyalty to the Byzantine emperor.

At the siege of Antioch, as the excerpt shows, Bohemund managed by any means possible to be the one to capture the city. Suddenly, he forgot his promise to the Byzantine emperor and kept the city for himself. Bohemund was one of the many Crusaders who came to fight the Muslims not so much for the Christian God as for his own benefit. He established the Principality of Antioch and did not bother accompanying the Crusaders as they later pushed on for Jerusalem.

Common Weal: Common good.

mentioned in Anna Comnena's account. With the spring came a new threat to the Crusaders, a Turkish army coming to help the people of Antioch. At this point, Stephen of Blois also decided to leave the battlefield. Meeting the Byzantine emperor on his way, Stephen told Alexius I of the desperate situation at Antioch, and the emperor turned back to Constantinople.

However, at Antioch matters improved for the Crusaders. A Muslim force coming to the aid of the city was met and defeated by the Franks and finally, on June 3, 1098, they took the city, killing all Muslim occupants. Then the Crusaders found themselves under siege when another Islamic force, under the Muslim leader Karbugah, attacked the city. Inspired by the discovery of what was supposed to be the lance that pierced the side of Jesus Christ as he died on the cross, the Crusaders rushed out of their fortified city on June 28 and defeated this Muslim army.

The ultimate goal of the First Crusade, liberating Jerusalem from Muslim control, was attained more than a year later when, on July 15, 1099, the western forces took that city and slaughtered all the Muslim inhabitants, including women and children. Jews also were included in the general massacre. After this victory, the Crusaders established the Latin Kingdom, a group of states set up in a narrow corridor along the Mediterranean Sea from Jerusalem to Antioch. Godfrey of Bouillon refused the title of king and, instead, became Defender of the Holy Sepulchre, or Christ's tomb. Those who followed him were less humble and became kings of Jerusalem. The Christians came into control of the Holy Land once again as a result of the First Crusade. However, this resulted in bad feelings between the Europeans and the Byzantine Empire. The Crusaders felt that the emperor had let them down, and the emperor for his part felt that the Crusaders had not kept their promise of loyalty to him. Instead of helping him get rid of the Turks, the Crusaders had created another power base with their Latin Kingdom, in direct competition with the Byzantine Empire. And Stephen of Blois, by the time he reached home, was met with general disapproval for deserting the battle. As the historian Hans Eberhard Mayer noted in *The Crusades,* Stephen's "wife's welcome home was anything but friendly."

Did you know...

- One of the four Crusader states created in the Middle East was Edessa, a Christian city occupied by the Turks. Baldwin, Godfrey of Bouillon's brother, freed that city even as the Crusaders were pushing on to Antioch. The County of Edessa became the first of the Crusader kingdoms to be established and Baldwin its first ruler.

- So many thousands were slaughtered by the Christian soldiers in Jerusalem that blood flowed ankle deep in the streets.

- News traveled slowly at the time of the Crusades. Pope Urban II, who had called for the First Crusade, died on July 29, 1099, before word arrived of the Crusaders' success. He never knew what events his words had inspired.

- Soon after the fall of Jerusalem, many of the knights and common soldiers in the Crusader army returned to Europe. The number left to protect the Holy Land shrank to only thousands. But those who stayed behind built well-fortified castles, and three religious orders of knights were formed as elite fighting forces: the Knights Hospitallers, the Knights Templar, and the Teutonic Knights. With these soldiers, the Europeans were able to hold on in the Holy Land for two centuries.

Consider the following...

- Explain some of the primary causes of the First Crusade (from the Western point of view).

- The Crusaders went to the Holy Land for a variety of reasons. Discuss some of the motivations of these Christian warriors.

- If, in 1097, you were a citizen of Constantinople—one of the most sophisticated and cosmopolitan cities of the world in its day—describe how you would feel to have the Crusaders arrive in your neighborhood.

For More Information

Books

Armstrong, Karen. *Holy War*. New York: Anchor, 2001.

Comnena, Anna. *The Alexiad*. Edited and translated by Elizabeth A. Dawes. London: Routledge, Kegan Paul, 1928.

Hindley, Geoffrey. *The Crusades: A History of Armed Pilgrimage and Holy War*. London: Constable, 2003.

Mayer, Hans Eberhard. *The Crusades*. 2nd ed. New York: Oxford University Press, 1988.

Munro, Dana C., ed. *Translations and Reprints from the Original Sources of European History*. Vol. 1. Philadelphia: University of Pennsylvania, 1896.

Web Sites

"The Crusades." *The ORB: On-line Reference Source for Medieval Studies.* http://the-orb.net/textbooks/westciv/1stcrusade.html (accessed on August 2, 2004).

"Internet Medieval Sourcebook: Crusader Letters." *Fordham University.* http://www.fordham.edu/halsall/source/cde-letters.html#Stephen (accessed on August 2, 2004).

"Internet Medieval Sourcebook: The Alexiad: Book XI." *Fordham University.* http://www.fordham.edu/halsall/basis/annacomnena-alexiad11.html (accessed on August 2, 2004).

Unforeseen Consequences

Excerpt from Chronicle of the Fourth Crusade and the
Conquest of Constantinople *(1207)*

**Originally written by Geoffrey de Villehardouin;
Translated by Frank T. Marzials; Published in 1908**

Excerpt from Chronica Regiae Coloniensis *(1213)*

**Reprinted in *The Crusades: A Documentary History*;
Translated by James Brundage; Published in 1962**

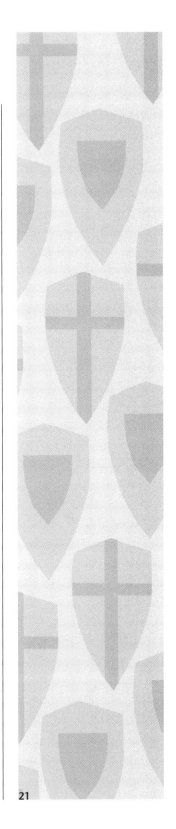

Numerous small Crusades took place throughout the
twelfth and into the thirteenth centuries. Quickly after
the First Crusade (1095–99), a smaller one was begun in 1101
to bring more troops to the Crusader states established in
Palestine, on the narrow seacoast of the eastern Mediterranean Sea. This effort failed, as did several other attempts to
send men. But the Crusaders were successful initially because
of the internal rivalries among the Muslims. The world of
Islam in the Middle East, made up of Arabs, Turks, Egyptians,
Kurds, and several other ethnic groups, did not present a
united front against the Christian invaders because they were
busy fighting one another. In addition to competing ethnic
groups, there also were competing branches of Islam. The
two major branches, Sunnis and Shiites, were as strong an
enemy to each other as they were to the Christians.

Slowly, though, the Muslims began to unite under
strong leaders, the first of whom was Zengi, the *atabeg*, or
governor, of Mosul in present-day Iraq. Zengi, a Seljuk Turk,
began to gather the Muslims under his leadership and then,
in 1144, captured the Crusader state of Edessa. For Zengi, the

fight against the Christians was a *jihad,* or holy war. This defeat for the Crusaders, in turn, brought about a new desire in Europe for a Crusade. Saint Bernard of Clairvaux preached such a new holy war to stop the rising power of Islam. Nobles, including King Louis VII of France and King Conrad III of Germany, took up the cross in the Second Crusade (1147–49), but their effort was a failure. They further damaged relations with the Byzantine Empire, and their complete defeat made the Muslims even bolder as they came to realize that they could beat the Christians.

Zengi was assassinated in 1146, before the Second Crusade, but his son, Nur al-Din, took his place in leading the Muslims of the Middle East against the Crusaders. One of Nur al-Din's generals invaded Egypt, and when he died, his nephew, Saladin, became leader of Egypt and further united the Muslim world. Saladin was perhaps the greatest military leader of the Islamic world, and when he captured Jerusalem from the Crusaders in 1187, he turned the tide against the Europeans. Unlike the aftermath of the Christian victory in 1099, the Muslims did not slaughter the inhabitants of the city. Instead, they let them go under a flag of truce. Though it took another century to drive the Franks out of the Holy Land, Saladin's victory at Jerusalem let the Christians know that it was only a matter of time until the Crusader states would be completely defeated.

As with Zengi's victory at Edessa, Saladin's at Jerusalem inspired a major Crusade. The Third Crusade (1189–91), led by England's Richard I the Lionheart, the king of France, and by the ruler of the Holy Roman Empire, managed to capture the port of Acre, but internal quarrels and too few fighting men led to overall failure. Richard I was able to win only a three-year truce from Saladin, which allowed Christian visitors to see the Holy Sepulchre in Jerusalem.

By the early thirteenth century, Pope Innocent III began calling for yet another Crusade in the Middle East. This time, however, the plan was to hit the Muslims in Egypt and then use the resources of that country to drive toward Jerusalem. The organization of transport was given to the Venetians, a major sea power at the time and one of the largest trading city-states of Europe. Political and business interests drove the Fourth Crusade (1202–04), and when the

Crusaders were unable to pay the Venetians the agreed-upon price for their transport, they were forced to become soldiers for hire, capturing Zara, a Christian city on the Yugoslavian coast that was causing Venice problems. This changed the entire direction of the Crusade, for after Zara the Christian army sailed to Constantinople, where, for a price, they agreed to install a young Byzantine prince on the throne of the Byzantine Empire. This action resulted in the sacking of Constantinople and the end of the Fourth Crusade; the Crusaders never got near the Muslims or the Holy Land.

Such unforeseen consequences also happened in 1212 with the two Children's Crusades, in which thousands of boys twelve years of age and younger took to the roads to battle in the Holy Land. The leaders, Stephen, a shepherd from France, and Nicholas, of Germany, were themselves boys and led their followers on an unhappy adventure that ended in misery and death for most.

A view of the center of Venice. The organization of transportation for the Fourth Crusade was given to the Venetians, a major sea power and one of the largest trading city-states of Europe. © *Archivo Iconografico, S.A./Corbis. Reproduced by permission.*

Things to Remember While Reading Excerpts about "Unforeseen Consequences of the Crusades":

- The First Crusade was the only successful Crusade for the Christians in the two centuries of conflict between Europe and the Middle East.

- Returning from the Third Crusade, Richard I, the Lionheart, was kidnapped by the German emperor and held prisoner until his mother, Eleanor of Aquitaine, could raise enough money from the British for his release. Eleanor was herself a veteran of the Second Crusade.

- The Crusader states developed much the same feudal structure as Europe had, with nobles staking out large areas of land that would be worked by those who promised loyalty to them. Within the first hundred years of their existence, the Crusader states were competing with one another. Peaceful Muslims found a place in such states, and many of the Europeans adopted Middle Eastern ways of dress and living.

- Geoffrey de Villehardouin was a knight and historian who took part in the Fourth Crusade, and his history of that event, written in French rather than Latin, is generally considered reliable. The *Chronica Regiae Coloniensis* is also assumed to be a real text from the time of the Children's Crusade, but many modern historians have questioned whether the participants were really young children or actually adults taking part in just one more failed mission to the Holy Land.

Excerpt from Chronicle of the Fourth Crusade and the Conquest of Constantinople

*Now give ear to one of the greatest marvels, and most wonderful adventures that you have ever heard tell of. At that time there was an emperor in Constantinople, whose name was Isaac, and he had a brother, Alexius by name, whom he had **ransomed** from cap-*

tivity among the Turks. This Alexius took his brother the emperor, tore the eyes out of his head, and made himself emperor by the aforesaid treachery. He kept Isaac a long time in prison, together with a son whose name was Alexius. This son escaped from prison, and fled in a ship to a city on the sea, which is called Ancona. Thence he departed to go to King Philip of Germany, who had his sister for wife; and he came to Verona in Lombardy, and lodged in the town, and found there a number of **pilgrims** and other people who were on their way to join the host [Crusader forces].

And those who had helped him to escape, and were with him, said: "Sire, here is an army in Venice, quite near to us, the best and most valiant people and knights that are in the world, and they are going overseas. Cry to them therefore for mercy, that they have pity on thee and on thy father, who have been so wrongfully **dispossessed**. And if they be willing to help thee, thou shalt be guided by them. **Perchance** they will take pity on thy **estate**." And Alexius said he would do this **right** willingly, and that the advice was good.

Thus he appointed **envoys**, and sent them to the Marquis Boniface of Montferrat, who was chief of the host, and to the other barons. And when the barons saw them, they marvelled greatly, and said to the envoys: "We understand right well what you tell us. We will send an envoy with the prince to King Philip, **whither** he is going. If the prince will help to recover the land overseas we will help him to recover his own land, for we know that it has been **wrested** from him and from his father wrongfully." So were envoys sent into Germany, both to the heir of Constantinople and to King Philip of Germany.

The barons consulted together on **the morrow** , and said that they would show the young Alexius, the son of the Emperor of Constantinople, to the people of the city. So they assembled all the **galleys**. The **Doge** of Venice and the **Marquis** of Montferrat entered into one,

French knight and historian Geoffrey de Villehardouin, who took part in the Fourth Crusade; his history of that event, written in French rather than Latin, is generally considered reliable.
© Bettman/Corbis. Reproduced by permission.

The Morrow: The next day.

Galleys: Ships

Doge: The title of the leader of Venice.

Marquis: A noble title, above a count and below a duke.

A mosaic showing the fall of Constantinople during the Fourth Crusade in 1204. *The Art Archive/Dagli Ort. Reproduced by permission.*

and took with them Alexius, the son of the Emperor Isaac; and into the other galleys entered the knights and barons, as many as would.

They went thus quite close to the walls of Constantinople and showed the youth to the people of the Greeks, and said, "Behold your natural lord; and be it known to you that we have not come to do you harm, but have come to guard and defend you, if so be that you return to your duty. For he whom you now obey as your lord holds rule by wrong and wickedness, against God and reason. And you know full well that he has dealt **treasonably** with him who is your lord and his brother, that he has blinded his eyes and [taken] from him his empire by wrong and wickedness. Now behold the rightful heir. If you hold with him, you will be doing as you ought; and if not we will do to you the very worst that we can." But for fear and terror of the Emperor Alexius, not one person on the land or in the city made show as if he held for the prince. So all went back to the host, and each sought his quarters ....

Now hear of a strange miracle: those who are within the city fly and abandon the walls, and the Venetians enter in, each as fast

Treasonably: Through disloyalty or betrayal, especially in the overthrow of a government.

and as best he can, and seize twenty-five of the towers, and man them with their people. And the Doge takes a boat, and sends messengers to the barons of the host to tell them that he has taken twenty-five towers, and that they may know for sooth that such towers cannot be retaken. The barons are so overjoyed that they cannot believe their ears; and the Venetians begin to send to the host in boats the horses and **palfreys** they have taken.

When the Emperor Alexius saw that our people had thus entered into the city, he sent his people against them in such numbers that our people saw they would be unable to endure the onset. So they set fire to the buildings between them and the Greeks; and the wind blew from our side, and the fire began to **wax** so great that the Greeks could not see our people who retired to the towers they had seized and conquered.

It seemed as if the whole plain was covered with troops, and they advanced slowly and in order. Well might we appear in **perilous case**, for we had but six **divisions**, while the Greeks had full forty, and there was not one of their divisions but was larger than any of ours. But ours were ordered in **such sort** that none could attack them save in front. And the Emperor Alexius rode so far forward that either side could shoot at the other. And when the Doge of Venice heard this, he made his people come forth, and leave the towers they had taken, and said he would live or die with the pilgrims. So he came to the camp, and was himself the first to land, and brought with him such of his people as he could.

Thus, for a long space, the armies of the pilgrims and of the Greeks stood one against the other; for the Greeks did not dare to throw themselves upon our ranks, and our people would not move from their **palisades**. And when the Emperor Alexius saw this, he began to withdraw his people, and when he had rallied them, he turned back....

Now listen to the miracles of our Lord—how gracious are they **whithersoever** it pleases Him to perform them! That very night the Emperor Alexius of Constantinople took of his treasure as much as he could carry, and took with him as many of his people as would go, and so fled and abandoned the city. And those of the city remained astonished, and they drew to the prison in which lay the Emperor Isaac, whose eyes had been put out. Him they clothed **imperially** , and bore to the great palace of Blachernae, and seated on a high throne; and there they did to him **obeisance** as their lord.

Palfreys: Saddle horses that are not warhorses.

Wax: Grow larger.

Perilous case: Dangerous position.

Divisions: Military units.

Such sort: Such a way.

Palisades: Fortified areas or enclosures or defensive walls made of wooden stakes.

Whithersoever: Wherever.

Imperially: Royally, with the clothing of a king.

Obeisance: A show of respect by bowing or other gestures.

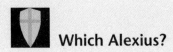

Which Alexius?

Alexius was a name taken by many of the emperors of the Byzantine Empire. Alexius I was the emperor who asked for help from Pope Urban II to fight the Seljuk Turks and thus brought on the First Crusade. That Alexius was a member of what was known as the Comnenan dynasty, the family line that ruled in Constantinople from 1081 to 1185. After the Comnenan dynasty came the Angelan dynasty, starting off with Isaac II, the emperor who was blinded by his ambitious brother. This brother who blinded Isaac became the emperor Alexius III, and he threw Isaac and Isaac's son, his own nephew, into prison to take power. Now this son of Isaac II was another Alexius, the one who escaped and ran off to Europe to get the Crusaders to help restore him and his father to power.

When the Crusaders chased off Alexius III, the new emperor became Alexius IV. (He ruled as coemperor with his father, Isaac, after the Crusaders conquered Constantinople, though he had the true power of the throne.) Soon, still another Alexius came into action, a distant relation to the Comnenan family. There were so many men named Alexius by this time that the Crusaders gave this one a nickname, "Murzuphlus," meaning "someone with thick eyebrows," for this man's eyebrows grew in a single strip over both eyes. Alexius Murzuphlus became Alexius V when he killed Alexius IV and put the poor old blind Isaac II back in prison to die. Alexius V did not maintain power for long; it was only a matter of two months until he was killed. He was the last Alexius to rule in Constantinople.

*Then they took messengers, by the advice of the Emperor Isaac, and sent them to the host, to **apprise** the son of the Emperor Isaac, and the barons, that the Emperor Alexius had fled, and that they had again raised up the Emperor Isaac as emperor....*

Excerpt from Chronica Regiae Coloniensis

*In this year occurred an outstanding thing and one much to be marveled at, for it is unheard of throughout the ages. About the time of Easter and **Pentecost** , without anyone having preached or called for it and prompted by I know not what spirit, many thousands of boys, ranging in age from six years to full maturity, left the plows or carts which they were driving, the flocks which they were pasturing, and anything else which they were doing. This they did despite the wishes of their parents, relatives, and friends who sought to make them draw back. Suddenly one ran after another to*

Apprise: Tell.

Pentecost: Christian festival on the seventh Sunday after Easter.

*take the cross. Thus, by groups of twenty, or fifty, or a hundred, they put up banners and began to journey to Jerusalem. They were asked by many people on whose advice or at whose urging they had set out upon this path. They were asked especially since only a few years ago many kings, a great many dukes, and innumerable people in powerful companies had gone there and had returned with the business unfinished. The present groups, moreover, were still of tender years and were neither strong enough nor powerful enough to do anything. Everyone, therefore, accounted them foolish and **imprudent** for trying to do this. They briefly replied that they were equal to the Divine will in this matter and that, whatever God might wish to do with them, they would accept it willingly and with humble spirit. They thus made some little progress on their journey. Some were turned back at Metz, others at Piacenza, and others even at Rome. Still others got to Marseilles, but whether they crossed to the Holy Land or what their end was is uncertain. One thing is sure: that of the many thousands who rose up, only very few returned.*

Imprudent: Unwise.

What happened next...

The Crusaders were able to put Alexius IV on the Byzantine throne, but once there he did not keep his end of the bargain. He had agreed to pay the Crusaders for putting him in power, but the money was not there, and the citizens of Constantinople did not want to pay higher taxes to raise the money. Then another Alexius came onto the scene and seized power in February 1204. He killed Alexius IV and made himself Alexius V and told the Crusaders to go home. The Crusaders were not going to leave without their payment. They needed the money to carry on the Crusade in the Holy Land. In April 1204 they began to attack Constantinople and captured the city, destroying much of it and killing thousands of its citizens. It was the worst destruction the city had ever seen. Then the Crusaders became caught up in forming the Latin Empire of Constantinople and never made it to the Holy Land.

Pope Innocent III excommunicated, or expelled, the Crusaders from the Catholic Church for these offenses against

An illustration of the Children's Crusade showing boys wearing robes with crosses. Some historians wonder if all of the facts surrounding the Children's Crusade are fact or fiction. *Corbis. Reproduced by permission.*

another Christian land, but the Crusader movement did not end with this shameful act. Instead, the energy and desire to fight for the Holy Land were taken up by the common people and by youths all over Europe. The Children's Crusade of 1212 was a result of such interest. Since the nobles did not gather for a new Crusade, the children took up the cause. A young French shepherd, Stephen of Cloyes, went to the French king, telling him he had a letter from God that instructed him to lead a Crusade. The king told the twelve-year-old to come back when he was grown up. But Stephen preached his message for a Crusade to other children in France and soon gathered thousands around him. They marched south toward the Mediterranean Sea and sailed off from the port of Marseilles, never to be heard of again. One later witness said that two of the ships sank and that the others were captured by pirates and the children sold into slavery.

Stephen's Crusade inspired a similar one by a twelve-year-old German boy, Nicholas, who gathered thousands of children but also some adults and marched over the Alpine mountain range to Rome. There, Pope Innocent III told them to go home, but many did not make it back to their homes, dying of starvation on the way. Some historians wonder if all the facts of the so-called Children's Crusade are true, but fact or fiction, this shows that the urge to go on a Crusade was still important in Europe at the beginning of the thirteenth century. The tragic Crusades of 1204 and 1212 would lead to further attempts to free the Holy Land from Muslim domination in three more major Crusades.

Did you know...

- During the attack on Constantinople, the Crusaders were in part led by the Venetian doge, or ruler, Enrico Dandolo, a man who was in his eighties. He personally led his forces into battle against the Byzantine defenders.

- Venice was the real winner of the Fourth Crusade, earning money from the Crusaders for transporting them to Constantinople and, at the same time, using the Crusader army to help them win new holdings in Asia Minor and in the Mediterranean as a result of the peace treaty with Constantinople.

- The Latin Empire of Constantinople lasted until 1261.

- Stephen of Cloyes's Children's Crusade supposedly had thirty thousand followers, all of whom died or were sold into slavery on their way to the Holy Land. The second group of young Crusaders led by the German, Nicholas, had almost twenty thousand followers. Only one-third of them survived the march to Rome.

Consider the following...

- What does the sack of Constantinople demonstrate about the motives of many of the Crusaders? Who was the enemy they were supposed to be fighting?

- The Children's Crusades were supposedly led by children. Discuss some of the arguments that you think these leaders used to recruit their adolescent armies.

• How old do you have to be to fight? The age for enlistment into the armed forces is eighteen; should younger children be allowed to join? Why or why not?

For More Information

Books

The Crusades: A Documentary History. Translated by James Brundage. Milwaukee, WI: Marquette University Press, 1962.

Hindley, Geoffrey. *The Crusades: A History of Armed Pilgrimage and Holy War.* London: Constable, 2003.

Mayer, Hans Eberhard. *The Crusades.* 2nd ed. New York: Oxford University Press, 1988.

Villehardouin, Geoffrey de. *Chronicles of the Fourth Crusade and the Conquest of Constantinople.* Translated by Frank Marzials. London: J. M. Dent, 1908.

Web Sites

"Chronica Regiae Coloniensis, s.a.1213. The 'Children's Crusade,' 1212." *Internet Medieval Sourcebook.* http://www.fordham.edu/halsall/source/1212pueri.html (accessed on August 2, 2004).

"The Crusades." *The ORB: On-line Reference Book for Medieval Studies.* http://the-orb.net/textbooks/westciv/1stcrusade.html (accessed on August 2, 2004).

"Memoirs or Chronicle of the Fourth Crusade and the Conquest of Constantinople." *Internet Medieval Sourcebook.* http://www.fordham.edu/halsall/basis/villehardouin.html (accessed on August 2, 2004).

The Gentle Art of Diplomacy

Excerpt from "Frederick II to Henry III of England," in Roger of Wendover's Flores Historiarum *(1229)*

Originally written by Frederick II; Reprinted in *Liber qui dictiur Flores Historiarum ab anno Domini MCLIV annoque Henrici Anglorum regis Secundi primo;* **Edited by H. G. Hewlett; Published in 1886–89**

Excerpt from Matthew Paris's Chronica Majora *(1258)*

Originally written by Gerold, Patriarch of Jerusalem; Reprinted in "Letters of the Crusaders," in *Translations and Reprints from the Original Sources of European History;* **Translated by Dana C. Munro; Published in 1896**

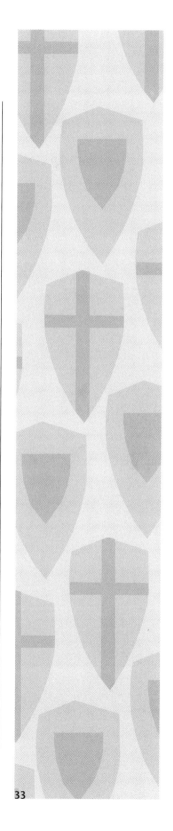

The disasters of the Fourth Crusade in 1204 and of the so-called Children's Crusade in 1212 left the Christian world worried about the fate of the Holy Land. Pope Innocent III continued to call for a new Crusade, but he died in 1216, before he could see that his attempts to gather a European army for a new holy war in Palestine had finally succeeded. Honorius III, who became the next pope, continued to write letters to the nobles calling for a Crusade. By 1217 enough German and French nobles had signed on for the expedition, which was planned to strike Egypt, take its main city of Cairo, and then use the resources of that kingdom to launch a strike at Jerusalem itself.

This Crusade, unlike earlier ones, was partly led by a church leader, Cardinal Pelagius, whom Honorius III sent as his personal representative. The main leader was, however, King John of Jerusalem, who ruled his very tiny kingdom from the Mediterranean port of Acre, almost totally surrounded by unfriendly Muslims. The Fifth Crusade lasted from 1218 to 1221 and was as unsuccessful as earlier ones conducted by the Christians. The Egyptian sultan (ruler), al-Malik al-Kamil,

Portrait of Frederick II, leader of the Sixth Crusade. Frederick regained Jerusalem from the Muslims without a battle by negotiating with Sultan al-Malik al-Kamil. © *Bettmann/Corbis. Reproduced by permission.*

managed to defeat the Crusaders at the Battle of Mansurah on the Nile River before they reached Cairo, despite an early Crusader victory at the town of Damietta. The Crusade was long and drawn out; Saint Francis of Assisi, founder of the Franciscan order of monks and church reformer, even made an appearance in 1219 to try to persuade al-Kamil to change religions and so end the battle. The Muslim declined the offer but was impressed with Francis's courage to put himself into the hands of the enemy.

With the failure of the Fifth Crusade, the church stopped sponsoring holy wars in the Middle East. The next two Crusades were funded by royalty, both the ruler of the Holy Roman Empire, Frederick II, and the king of France, Louis IX. Frederick II had long been an enemy of church power and delayed entering the Fifth Crusade long enough to entirely miss the action. But he had made a promise to go on a Crusade, and he had to keep the promise. This promise resulted in the Sixth Crusade (1228–29). Frederick II was, however, a very intelligent ruler, as talented in international relations as he was with the sword. He was determined to go on a Crusade in 1228, but before leaving Europe, he was in communication with the Egyptian sultan, al-Kamil, with the offer of a deal. If the Muslim would turn over Jerusalem to the Christians, Frederick II guaranteed a long period of peace. This was important for al-Kamil, who was involved in power battles with other Muslims for control of Syria. For Frederick II such a bloodless victory would be a great boost in his continual fight for dominance in Europe over the Catholic Church.

Matters were largely arranged by letter even before Frederick II set out with his small Crusader force for the Holy Land: Jerusalem would change hands. Still, when it happened, there were those among the Crusaders who were not happy with the arrangement. They thought that Frederick II and the army could have won more from the Muslims, who were at a weak point in 1228. They believed that the emperor could have won back more of the Holy Land if only he had been willing to fight.

Things to Remember While Reading Excerpts about the Sixth Crusade:

- Frederick II not only was emperor of the Holy Roman Empire in 1228 when he went on the Sixth Crusade but, through his recent marriage to a fourteen-year-old girl named Yolanda, he also had a claim to become king of Jerusalem and thus make his empire even larger and stronger.

- When he went on Crusade, Frederick II was twice excommunicated, or expelled, from the Catholic Church for previously failing to go on Crusade, as he had promised.

- Frederick was opposed in his mission by the patriarch (Eastern Orthodox religious leader) of Jerusalem, Gerold of Valence, who started a campaign against him.

- Sultan al-Malik al-Kamil had much to gain and little to lose by returning Jerusalem to the Christians. The city's walls had been destroyed not long before, and it was not defensible. It would also be surrounded by Muslims, who could take the city back at any moment. Additionally, two Muslim holy places inside Jerusalem, the Dome of the Rock and al-Aqsa Mosque, an Islamic place of worship, were left in Muslim hands.

- Al-Kamil was as good a bargainer as Frederick II. He knew of the difficulties between Frederick and the patriarch and so slowed down talks about a treaty to put the pressure on Frederick. In the end, he gained more than he had hoped. His keeping Muslim shrines inside Jerusalem especially angered the patriarch, Gerold, and made relations between Frederick and the church even worse than before.

- Frederick II crowned himself king of Jerusalem in the Church of the Holy Sepulchre in Jerusalem on March 18, 1229, one day before the arrival of a church official, who had been sent by Gerold to stop all religious services in the city.

- In both the following letters, from Frederick II to Henry III and from the patriarch Gerold to the faithful, al-Kamil is referred to as the "sultan of Babylon." He was, however, at that time the sultan of Egypt and would only later rule Damascus and Babylon.

Excerpt from "Frederick II to Henry III of England"

*Frederic, by the grace of God, the **august** emperor of the Romans, king of Jerusalem and Sicily, to his well-beloved friend, Henry, king of the English, health and sincere affection.*

*Let all rejoice and **exult** in the Lord, and let those who are correct in heart glorify **Him**, who, to make known His power, does not make boast of horses and chariots, but has now gained glory for Himself, in the scarcity of His soldiers, that all may know and understand that He is glorious in His majesty, terrible in His magnificence, and wonderful in His plans on the sons of men, changing seasons at will, and bringing the hearts of different nations together; for in these few days, by a miracle rather than by strength that business has been brought to a conclusion, which for a length of time past many chiefs and rulers of the world amongst the multitude of nations, have never been able till now to accomplish by force, however great, nor by fear.*

Not, therefore, to keep you in suspense by a long account, we wish to inform your holiness, that we, firmly putting our trust in God, and believing that Jesus Christ, His Son, in whose service we have so devotedly exposed our bodies and lives, would not abandon us in these unknown and distant countries, but would at least give us wholesome advice and assistance for His honor, praise, and glory, boldly in the name set forth from Acre on the fifteenth day of the month of November last past and arrived safely at Joppa, intending to rebuild the castle at that place with proper strength, that afterwards the approach to the holy city of Jerusalem might be not only easier, but also shorter and more safe for us as well as for all Christians. When, therefore we were, in the confidence of our trust in God, engaged at Joppa, and superintending the building of the castle and

August: Inspiring respect.

Exult: Triumph, express joy.

Him: God, referred to by the capitalized third-person singular masculine pronoun.

The Crusades: Primary Sources

the cause of Christ, as necessity required and as was our duty, and **whilst** all our **pilgrims** were busily engaged in these matters, several messengers often passed to and fro between us and the **sultan** of Babylon; for he and another sultan, called Xaphat, his brother were with a large army at the city of Gaza, distant about one day's journey from us; in another direction, in the city of Sichen, which is commonly called Neapolis, and situated in the plains, the sultan of Damascus his nephew, was staying with an immense number of knights and soldiers also about a day's journey from us and the Christians.

And whilst the treaty was in progress between the parties on either side of the restoration of the Holy Land, at length Jesus Christ, the Son of God, beholding from on high our devoted endurance and patient devotion to His cause, in His merciful compassion of us, at length brought it about that the sultan of Babylon restored to us the holy city, the place where the feet of Christ trod, and where the true worshippers adore the Father in spirit and in truth. But that we may inform you of the particulars of this surrender each as they happened, be it known to you that not only is the body of the **aforesaid** city restored to us, but also the whole of the country extending from thence to the seacoast near the castle of Joppa, so that for the future pilgrims will have free passage and a safe return to and from the **sepulchre**; provided, however, that the **Saracens** of that part of the country, since they hold the temple in great **veneration**, may come there as often as they choose in the character of pilgrims, to worship according to their custom, and that we shall **henceforth** permit them to come, however, only as many as we may choose to allow, and without arms, nor are they to dwell in the city, but outside, and as soon as they have paid their devotions they are to depart.

Moreover, the city of Bethlehem is restored to us, and all the country between Jerusalem and that city; as also the city of Nazareth, and all the country between Acre and that city; the whole of the district of Turon, which is very extensive, and very advantageous to the Christians; the city of Sidon, too, is given up to us with the whole plain and its **appurtenances**, which will be the

Front view of a gold coin bearing the image of Frederick II. Frederick crowned himself king of Jerusalem after negotiating the return of Jerusalem to Christians during the Sixth Crusade.
© *Gianni Dagli Orti/Corbis. Reproduced by permission.*

Whilst: While.

Pilgrims: Religious visitors or travelers.

Sultan: Ruler, leader.

Aforesaid: Mentioned before.

Sepulchre: Tomb, burial place; in this case the tomb of Jesus Christ in Jerusalem.

Saracens: Term used by Europeans for all Muslims.

Veneration: Respect or reverence.

Henceforth: From now on.

Appurtenances: Attachments, connected areas.

more acceptable to the Christians the more advantageous it has till now appeared to be to the Saracens, especially as there is a good harbor there, and from there great quantities of arms and necessaries might be carried to the city of Damascus and often from Damascus to Babylon. And although according to our treaty we are allowed to rebuild the city of Jerusalem in as good a state as it has ever been, and also the castles of Joppa, Cesarea, Sidon, and that of St. Mary of the Teutonic order, which the brothers of that order have begun to build in the mountainous district of Acre, and which it has never been allowed the Christians to do during any former truce; nevertheless the sultan is not allowed, till the end of the truce between him and us, which is agreed on for ten years, to repair or rebuild any fortresses or castles.

And so on Sunday, the eighteenth day of February last past, which is the day on which Christ, the Son of God, rose from dead, and which, in memory of His **resurrection**, is solemnly cherished and kept holy by all Christians in general throughout the world, this treaty of peace was confirmed by oath between us. Truly then on us and on all does that day seem to have shone favorably, in which the angels sing in praise of God, "Glory to God on high, and on earth peace, and goodwill toward men." And in acknowledgment of such great kindness and of such an honor, which, beyond our **deserts** and contrary to the opinion of many, God has mercifully **conferred** on us, to the lasting **renown** of His compassion, and that in His holy place we might personally offer to Him the **burnt offering** of our lips, be it known to you that on the seventeenth day of the month of March […], we, in company with all the pilgrims who had with us faithfully followed Christ, the Son of God, entered the holy city of Jerusalem, and after worshipping at the holy sepulchre, we, as being a Catholic emperor, on the following day, wore the crown, which Almighty God provided for us from the throne of His majesty, when of His especial grace, He **exalted** us on high amongst the princes of the world; so that whilst we have supported the honor of this high dignity, which belongs to us by right of sovereignty, it is more and more evident to all that the hand of the Lord hath done all this; and since His mercies are over all His works, let the worshippers of the **orthodox faith** henceforth know and relate it far and wide throughout the world, that He, who is blessed for ever, has visited and redeemed His people, and has raised up the horn of salvation for us in the house of His servant David.

And before we leave the city of Jerusalem, we have determined magnificently to rebuild it, and its towers and walls, and we intend

Resurrection: Rising from the dead or being reborn.

Deserts: That which is deserved or owing.

Conferred: Granted, awarded.

Renown: Fame, recognition.

Burnt offering: A sacrifice to God, often an animal, burned at an altar; here used to mean words of praise.

Exalted: Praised, raised in rank.

Orthodox faith: True religion, here referring to Christianity.

so to arrange matters that, during our absence, there shall be no less care and diligence used in the business, than if we were present in person. In order that this our present letter may be full of **exultation** throughout, and so a happy end correspond with its happy beginning, and rejoice your royal mind, we wish it to be known to you our ally, that the said sultan is bound to restore to us all those captives whom he did not in **accordance** with the treaty made between him and the Christians deliver up at the time when he lost Damietta some time since, and also the others who have been since taken.

Given at the holy city of Jerusalem, on the seventeenth day of the month of March, in the year of our Lord one thousand two hundred and twenty-nine.

Excerpt from "Gerold to All the Faithful"

Gerold, **patriarch** of Jerusalem, to all the faithful greeting.

If it should be fully known how astonishing, **nay** rather, **deplorable**, the conduct of the emperor has been in the eastern lands from beginning to end, to the great **detriment** of the cause of Jesus Christ and to the great injury of the Christian faith, from the sole of his foot to the top of his head no common sense would be found in him. For he came, **excommunicated**, without money and followed by scarcely forty knights, and hoped to maintain himself by **spoiling** the inhabitants of Syria. He first came to Cyprus and there most discourteously seized that nobleman J. [John] of Ibelin and his sons, whom he had invited to his table under **pretext** of speaking of the affairs of the Holy Land. Next the king, whom he had invited to meet him, he retained almost as a captive. He thus by violence and fraud got possession of the kingdom.

After these achievements he passed over into Syria. Although in the beginning he promised to do marvels, and although in the presence of the foolish he boasted loudly, he immediately sent to the sultan of Babylon [al-Kamil] to demand peace. This conduct **rendered** him **despicable** in the eyes of the sultan and his subjects, especially after they had discovered that he was not at the head of a numerous army, which might have to some extent added weight to his words. Under the pretext of defending Joppa, he marched with the Christian army towards that city, in order to be nearer the sultan and in order to be able more easily to treat of peace or obtain a truce. What more shall I say? After long and mysterious conferences, and without having consulted any one who lived in the country, he suddenly announced one day that he had made peace with the sul-

Exultation: Triumph, great joy.

Accordance: Conforming with.

Patriarch: One of the four main religious leaders of the Eastern Orthodox Church.

Nay: No.

Deplorable: Very bad.

Detriment: Negative effect.

Excommunicated: Expelled from the church.

Spoiling: Plundering, stealing from.

Pretext: A false reason.

Rendered: Made.

Despicable: Hated, beneath contempt.

tan. No one saw the text of the peace or truce when the emperor took the oath to observe the **articles** which were agreed upon. Moreover, you will be able to see clearly how great the **malice** was and how **fraudulent** the **tenor** of certain articles of the truce which we have decided to send to you. The emperor, for giving credit to his word, wished as a guarantee only the word of the sultan, which he obtained. For he said, among other things, that the holy city was surrendered to him.

He went **thither** with the Christian army on the eve of the Sunday when "Oculi mei" is sung [third Sunday in Lent, or the period before Easter]. The Sunday following, without any fitting ceremony and although excommunicated, in the chapel of the sepulchre of our Lord, to the **manifest** prejudice of his honor and of the imperial dignity he put the **diadem** upon his forehead, although the **Saracens** still held the temple of the Lord and Solomon's temple, and although they proclaimed publicly as before the law of Mohammed to the great confusion and **chagrin** of the pilgrims.

This same prince, who had previously very often promised to fortify Jerusalem, departed in secrecy from the city at dawn on the following Monday. The **Hospitalers and the Templars** promised solemnly and earnestly to aid him with all their forces and their advice, if he wanted to fortify the city, as he had promised. But the emperor, who did not care to set affairs right, and who saw that there was no certainty in what had been done, and that the city in the state in which it had been surrendered to him could be neither defended nor fortified, was content with the name of surrender, and on the same day hastened with his family to Joppa. The pilgrims who had entered Jerusalem with the emperor, witnessing his departure, were unwilling to remain behind.

The following Sunday when "Laetare Jerusalem" is sung [fourth Sunday in Lent], he arrived at Acre. There in order to **seduce** the people and to obtain their favor, he granted them a certain privilege. God knows the motive which made him act thus, and his subsequent conduct will make it known. As, moreover, the passage was near, and as all pilgrims, humble and great, after having visited the Holy Sepulchre, were preparing to withdraw, as if they had accomplished their pilgrimage, because no truce had been concluded with the sultan of Damascus, we, seeing that the holy land was already deserted and abandoned by the pilgrims, in our council formed the plan of retaining soldiers for the common good, by means of the **alms** given by the king of France of holy memory.

Articles: Terms, conditions (of the truce).

Malice: Ill will.

Fraudulent: Fake.

Tenor: General meaning.

Thither: In that direction, to that place.

Manifest: Obvious.

Diadem: Crown.

Saracens: Christian term for Muslims.

Chagrin: Sorrow and shame.

Hospitalers/Hospitallers and the Templars: Fighting orders of the church.

Seduce: Persuade to do something.

Alms: Donated money.

Convoked: Called together.

Prelates: High religious officials.

When the emperor heard of this, he said to us that he was astonished at this, since he had concluded a truce with the sultan of Babylon. We replied to him that the knife was still in the wound, since there was not a truce or peace with the sultan of Damascus, nephew of the aforesaid sultan and opposed to him, adding that even if the sultan of Babylon was unwilling, the former could still do us much harm. The emperor replied, saying that no soldiers ought to be retained in his kingdom without his advice and consent, as he was now king of Jerusalem. We answered to that, that in the matter in question, as well as in all of a similar nature, we were very sorry not to be able, without endangering the salvation of our souls, to obey his wishes, because he was excommunicated. The emperor made no response to us, but on the following day he caused the pilgrims who inhabited the city to be assembled outside by the public crier, and by special messengers he also **convoked** the **prelates** and the monks.

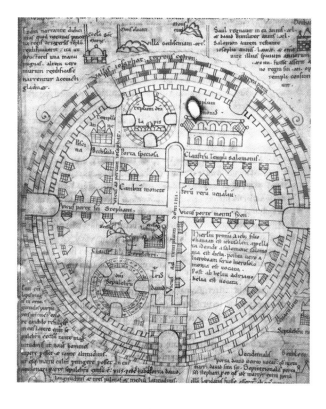

A circular plan of Jerusalem showing the Holy Sepulchre and the Temple of Solomon. Gerold, the patriarch of Jerusalem condemned the retaking of the city by Frederick II during the Sixth Crusade. *By permission of The British Library (Add. 32343).*

Addressing them in person, be began to complain bitterly of us, by heaping up false accusations. Then turning his remarks to the **venerable** master of the Templars he publicly attempted to severely **tarnish** the reputation of the latter, by various vain speeches, seeking thus to throw upon others the responsibility for his own faults which were now manifest, and adding at last, that we were maintaining troops with the purpose of injuring him. After that he ordered all foreign soldiers, of all nations, if they valued their lives and property, not to remain in the land from that day on, and ordered count Thomas, whom he intended to leave as **bailiff** of the country, to punish with **stripes** any one who was found **lingering**, in order that the punishment of one might serve as an example to many. After doing all this he withdrew, and would listen to no excuse or answers to the charges which he had so shamefully made. He determined immediately to post some **crossbowmen** at the gates of the city, ordering them to allow the Templars to go out but not to return. Next he fortified with crossbows the churches and other elevated positions and especially those which commanded the communications between

Venerable: Respected.

Tarnish: Damage.

Bailiff: Sheriff.

Stripes: Lashes of the whip.

Lingering: Remaining behind.

Crossbowmen: Soldiers equipped with crossbows, a medieval weapon.

the Templars and ourselves. And you may be sure that he never showed as much animosity and hatred against Saracens.

For our part, seeing his **manifest** wickedness, we assembled all the prelates and all the pilgrims, and **menaced** with excommunication all those who should aid the emperor with their advice or their services against the Church, the Templars, the other monks of the Holy Land, or the pilgrims.

The emperor was more and more irritated, and immediately caused all the passages to be guarded more strictly, refused to allow any kind of provisions to be brought to us or to the members of our party, and placed everywhere crossbowmen and archers, who attacked severely us, the Templars and the pilgrims. Finally to fill the measure of his malice, he caused some **Dominicans and Minorites** [Franciscans] who had come on **Palm Sunday** to the proper places to announce the Word of God, to be torn from the pulpit, to be thrown down and dragged along the ground and whipped throughout the city, as if they had been robbers. Then seeing that he did not obtain what he had hoped from the above-mentioned siege he treated of peace. We replied to him that we would not hear of peace until he sent away the crossbowmen and other troops, until he had returned our property to us, until finally he had restored all things to the condition and freedom in which they were on the day when he entered Jerusalem. He finally ordered what we wanted to be done, but it was not executed. Therefore we placed the city under **interdict**.

The emperor, realizing that his wickedness could have no success, was unwilling to remain any longer in the country. And, as if he would have liked to ruin everything, he ordered the crossbows and engines of war, which for a long time had been kept at Acre for the defense of the Holy Land, to be secretly carried on his **vessels**. He also sent away several of them to the sultan of Babylon, as his dear friend. He sent a troop of soldiers to Cyprus to **levy** heavy contributions of money there, and, what appeared to us more astonishing, he destroyed the **galleys** which he was unable to take with him. Having learned this, we resolved to **reproach** him with it, but shunning the **remonstrance** and the correction, he entered a galley secretly, by an **obscure** way, on the day of the Apostles St. Philip and St. James, and hastened to reach the island of Cyprus, without saying adieu to any one, leaving Joppa **destitute**; and may he never return!

Very soon the bailiffs of the above-mentioned sultan shut off all departure from Jerusalem for the Christian poor and the Syrians, and many pilgrims died thus on the road.

Manifast Clear; obvious.

Menaced: Threatened.

Dominicans and Minorites: Catholic religious orders or groups.

Palm Sunday: The Sunday before Easter.

Interdict: A church censure, or official decree of disapproval.

Vessels: Ships.

Levy: Collect, as a tax.

Galleys: Ships with sails.

Reproach: Express disapproval of.

Remonstrance: Words of protest.

Obscure: Hidden.

Destitute: Poor, needy

Preserving Knowledge

We are able to gain insights into long-ago times because people kept records of what happened. In modern days we call such people historians. In addition to their work, the modern media, such as television and radio, record almost every event that happens. In today's world, some might say that there is too much "history." But in the time of men like Frederick II and the patriarch Gerold, the job of recording events was left mostly to Christian monks, or members of religious orders living in monasteries outside regular society. These monks kept detailed accounts of happenings in the world in works called "chronicles."

Some of the best of these medieval chronicles were kept by monks in one English monastery near London, called Saint Albans. Members of the Benedictine religious order, these monks went in for the big sweep of history. Roger of Wendover, author of the *Flores Historiarum* ("Flowers of History"), laid out the history of the world from the creation to 1235. It is in his work that Frederick's letter to the king of England is preserved. Another chronicler of Saint Albans, Matthew Paris, wrote a bit later than Roger. His *Chronica Majora* looks at the history of the world from the Creation up to 1259 and includes the letter of Gerold to the "faithful," or members of the Eastern Orthodox religion. An artist as well as a historian, Matthew illustrated his own manuscripts. The work of these early English historians, or chroniclers, was gathered and edited in the nineteenth century in an enormous publishing project called the Rolls Series, which preserves medieval history for the modern world.

*This is what the emperor did, to the **detriment** of the Holy Land and of his own soul, as well as many other things which are known and which we leave to others to relate. May the merciful God **deign** to soften the results! Farewell.*

Detriment: Harm.

Deign: Consent, agree.

What happened next...

The treaty signed between Frederick II and the sultan al-Kamil gave both sides certain advantages. Yet both the emperor and sultan were surprised by the anger such a treaty caused. The church and other Crusaders complained that Frederick II did not go far enough or that he bargained away his advantage. At the same time, other Muslims were shocked that al-Kamil, who was supposed to be the protector of Islam, would give Jerusalem back to the Christians, even if Islam did keep control of its most important holy sites in the city.

Both leaders survived the storm of criticism, though. Frederick II was forced to return to Italy to protect part of his empire that had come under attack by armies of the pope. He continued to battle the power of the church until his death in 1250. Al-Kamil used the time of truce with the Crusaders to fight his opponents among the Muslims. He took Damascus and secured his power in Syria. Then he became the protector of Islam against a new enemy, the Mongols, who were beginning to invade the region from their home in Central Asia. The sultan al-Kamil died in 1238, tired out from a life of fighting the enemies of Islam.

Jerusalem stayed in Christian hands until it was sacked in 1244 by Turkish Muslims. This, in turn, led to the Seventh Crusade (1248–54), the last of the large-scale military adventures by Crusaders in the Middle East. Frederick II changed the way Europeans thought about the Crusades. If he could win by diplomacy, or negotiation, what others had failed to win by war, what was the purpose of fighting? This question took some of the enthusiasm out of the Crusader movement.

Did you know…

- Frederick II actually used his Crusader army in the Sixth Crusade not against the Muslims but to bully the Christians in the Holy Land to support him as king of Jerusalem. Some historians say that Frederick's goal was not the conquest of Muslim-held territories in Palestine but the takeover of the Crusader states there.

- Frederick II was one of the best-educated emperors of the day. He was a fan of Islamic scholarship and art, having grown up in Sicily, where Arabs had once been in power. He was nicknamed "Wonder of the World," founded a university, organized his government along modern models, and was himself an amateur scientist.

- Frederick II shocked the Christian faithful in Jerusalem by visiting Muslim shrines.

- At the time of the Sixth Crusade a new enemy to both Christians and Muslims was sweeping down from the north into the Middle East. The Mongols, a nomadic warrior tribe, conquered northern China in 1212 and had become the rulers of Central Asia by 1222. In the 1230s they occupied Russia, Ukraine, Poland, and Hungary. Both Christian Europe and the Muslim Middle East were next on their agenda.

Consider the following…

- Who do you think was the real winner of the Sixth Crusade, Frederick II or al-Kamil? Why?

- If important issues, such as the handover of Jerusalem to the Christians in the Sixth Crusade, could be solved without bloodshed, why do you think the wars continued between Christians and Muslims during the Crusades?

- Discuss some reasons why the Crusader states in the Holy Land might not have been behind Frederick II and his Sixth Crusade.

For More Information

Books

Hindley, Geoffrey. *The Crusades: A History of Armed Pilgrimage and Holy War.* London: Constable, 2003.

Mayer, Hans Eberhard. *The Crusades.* 2nd ed. New York: Oxford University Press, 1988.

Munro, Dana C., trans. "Letters of the Crusades." *Translations and Reprints from the Original Sources of European History.* Philadelphia: University of Pennsylvania, 1896.

Powell, James M. *Anatomy of a Crusade, 1213–1221.* Philadelphia: University of Pennsylvania Press, 1986.

Roger of Wendover. *Liber qui dictiur Flores Historiarum ab anno Domini MCLIV annoque Henrici Anglorum regis Secundi primo.* Edited by H. G. Hewlett. 3 vols. London: Rolls Series, 1886–1889.

Web Sites

"The Crusades." *The ORB: On-line Reference Book for Medieval Studies.* http://the-orb.net/textbooks/westciv/1stcrusade.html (accessed on August 3, 2004).

Fordham University. "Frederick II's Crusade: Letters, 1229." *Internet Medieval Sourcebook.* http://www.fordham.edu/halsall/source/fred2c delets.html (accessed on August 3, 2004).

The Final Good-Bye

Excerpt from "The Capture of Jerusalem, 1244,"
in Matthew of Paris's Chronica Majora *(1258)*

Originally written by Master of the Hospitallers at Jerusalem, Tolord de Melaye; Reprinted in "Letters of the Crusaders," *Translations and Reprints from the Original Sources of European History*; Translated by Dana C. Munro; Published in 1896

Excerpt from "The Fall of Acre, 1291,"
in Description of the Holy Land and the Way Thither *(1350)*

Originally written by Ludolph of Suchem; Reprinted in *The Crusades: A Documentary History*; Edited by James Brundage; Published in 1962

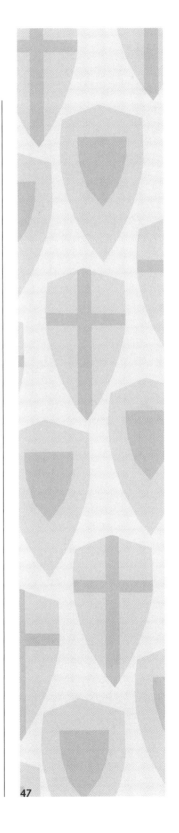

The thirteenth century brought an end to the Crusader states in the Holy Land. These Christian kingdoms had held on from their creation in 1099 by a combination of aid from Europe; military strength provided by their fighting religious orders, such as the Knights Templar and Knights Hospitallers; and a complex policy of playing off one Muslim enemy against another. The Crusaders, who at the time of the First Crusade were angry at Alexius I of the Byzantine Empire for his tricky dealings with the Muslims, had learned such lessons well over the years. They became very good at double-dealing as well, making treaties with one group of Muslims in order to hurt another, stronger group. There was even talk of making an alliance with the Mongols, that warrior-like tribe from Central Asia that was tearing the Middle East apart in the thirteenth century.

However, the Crusaders were not just playing politics against the Muslims; they were also battling each other. As the size of the Crusader states grew smaller and smaller under pressure from Muslim fighters, the Crusaders began turning against one another, fighting over territory and policy. They even imported conflicts from Europe, as seen in the following selections. The divisions between the various Muslim groups, caused by family or dynasty, and the competing branches of Islam had allowed the Crusaders to capture the Holy Land in the first place. Now the Crusaders were becoming as divided as the Muslims had been, with one state or city making treaties with the Turks or the Egyptians so that they could better compete against another Crusader state.

Of the four original states, the County of Edessa, the County of Tripoli, the Kingdom of Jerusalem, and the Principality of Antioch, little remained by the twelfth century, and it was in much weakened condition. Edessa was lost to the Muslims in 1144, and part of it was sold off to the Byzantine Empire. Jerusalem was lost in 1187 but won back by Frederick II in 1229 by treaty rather than war. That situation would also change, as shown in the following letter from the master, or chief, Hospitaller of Jerusalem describing the sack of the city by a Turkish Muslim force. After 1244 it was all downhill for the Crusaders. The central city for the Kingdom of Jerusalem became the fortified port of Acre, and, to the north, Tripoli and Antioch joined together under one leader. Smaller cities, such as Beirut and Tyre, also were fortified and held on until the very end against the Muslims, as did some of the famous forts, such as Krak des Chevaliers of the Hospitallers.

The fall of Jerusalem in 1244 contributed to the mounting of the last great Crusade to the Holy Land. The Seventh Crusade (1248–54), led by France's Louis IX, struck in Egypt, as had the Fifth Crusade. Like that earlier one, it, too, was a failure for the Christians. But from the Muslim point of view, it signaled the rebirth of Islam. Out of the chaos of that Crusade was born the Mamluk, or slave, dynasty of Egypt, a ruling line that lasted for several centuries and that unified much of the Middle East. These Mamluks were of mostly Turkish origin and were raised as professional soldiers. By 1260 they had become so powerful that they took over Egypt from their former masters. Led by the famous military ruler Baybars, the Mamluks drove the Crusaders into an ever-smaller corner of the Middle East. First, however, they had to deal with the Mongols, who sacked Baghdad in 1258 and were threatening the entire Middle East. The Mamluks defeated the Mongols at the Battle of Ayn Jalut in 1260, and then Baybars was free to turn his armies against the Christians. Antioch fell in 1268, and all its defenders were slaughtered. Baybars was no Saladin; although he was as great a general, he did not fight like a gentleman. Women, children, and men alike were killed without mercy.

After his death in 1277, leadership of the Mamluks was taken over by the general Kalavun, who continued to battle both the Crusaders and the Mongols. Kalavun made treaties when necessary and sent his troops into battle when such diplomacy did not work, taking Tripoli by force in 1289. By 1291 his son, al-Ashraf al-Khalil, had taken over as sultan of Egypt and gathered a huge Muslim force of about sixty thousand cavalry (horse-mounted soldiers) and about twice as many foot soldiers at the walls of the last great Crusader city, Acre. This was to be the final curtain for the Crusaders.

Things to Remember While Reading Excerpts about "The Final Good-Bye":

- Although Jerusalem was given back to the Christian Crusaders in 1229, it was impossible to fortify, for the old walls had been destroyed. To secure its position, the Kingdom of Jerusalem made a treaty with the Muslim rulers of Damascus, Syria, who were in conflict with the sultan of Egypt. When these two states went to war with each other, Jerusalem was caught in the middle. The Egyptians hired a tribe of Turks, the Khwarismians, to fight along with them, and these Turks swept into the Holy Land, capturing Jerusalem in 1244.

- The fall of Jerusalem in 1244 brought about the Seventh Crusade, which, in turn, helped create the powerful Mamluk dynasty in Egypt.

- So divided had the Crusaders become in the late thirteenth century that historians note that it was competing Crusaders who urged the Mamluk sultan Kalavun to attack Tripoli in 1289.

- The Crusaders finally united at the threat to Acre, their last stronghold. The military orders gathered their troops there and were aided by soldiers from England, France, and Italy, but it was a situation of having done too little and too late.

- When laying siege to Acre, the Muslims decided that they could not break through the thick walls of the fortified city. Instead, they brought in "sappers," (miners) who dug under the walls, weakening them and ultimately causing them to cave in.

- Written seventy years after the fact, Ludolph of Suchem's account of the fall of Acre in 1291 should be read with care. Like all good travel writers, Ludolph liked to exaggerate and change history for dramatic purposes. His timeline is generally accurate, but his numbers of Islamic soldiers is greatly exaggerated.

Excerpts from
"The Capture of Jerusalem, 1244"

To the most **potent** lord, M. de Melaye, brother G. of Newcastle, by the grace of God, **humble** master of the holy house at Jerusalem, and guardian of the poor followers of Christ greeting.

From the information contained in our letters, which we have sent to you on each passage, you can plainly enough see how ill the business of the Holy Land has proceeded, on account of the opposition which for a long time existed, at the time of making the truce, respecting the **espousing** of the cause of the Damascenes against the sultan of Babylon; and now wishing your excellency to be informed of other events since **transpired**, we have thought it worth our while to inform you that, about the beginning of the summer last past, the **sultan** of Damascus, and Seisser, sultan of Cracy, who were formerly enemies, made peace and entered into a treaty with the Christians, on the following conditions; namely, that they should restore to the Christians the whole of the kingdom of Jerusalem, and the territory which had been in the possession of the Christians, near the river Jordan, besides some villages which they retained possession of in the mountains, and that the Christians were faithfully to give them all the assistance in their power in attacking the sultan of Babylon.

The terms of this treaty having been agreed to by both parties the Christians began to take up their **abode** in the Holy City, whilst their army remained at Gazara, in company with that of the aforesaid sultan's, to **harass** the sultan of Babylon. After they had been some time engaged in that undertaking, **patriarch** of Jerusalem landed [...], and, after taking some slight bodily rest, he was inspired with a longing to visit the **sepulchre** of our Lord, and set out on that pilgrimage, on which we also accompanied him. After our vow of pilgrimage was fulfilled, we heard in the **Holy City** that a countless multitude of that barbarous and **perverse** race, called **Choermians**, had, at the summons and order of the sultan of Babylon, occupied the whole surface of the country in the furthest part of our territories adjoining Jerusalem, and had put every living soul to death by fire and sword.

A council was on this held by the Christians living at Jerusalem, and ... it was **prudently** arranged that all the inhabitants of the

Potent: Powerful.

Humble: Modest, not important.

Espousing: Supporting.

Transpired: Took place, happened.

Sultan: Ruler.

Abode: Residence.

Harass: Make small attacks to wear down an enemy.

Patriarch: Religious leader of the Eastern Orthodox Church.

Sepulchre: Tomb.

Holy City: Jerusalem.

Perverse: Wicked.

Choermians: A Turkish tribe, also known as the Khwarismians or the Khorezmians.

Prudently: Demonstrating careful thought.

*Holy City of both sexes and of every age, should proceed, under escort of a **battalion** of our knights, to Joppa, as a place of safety and refuge.... After finishing our deliberations, we led the people cautiously out of the city, and had proceeded confidently half the distance, when, owing to the intervention of our old and wily enemy, the devil, a most destructive obstacle presented itself to us; for the aforesaid people raised on the walls of the city some **standards**, which they found left behind by the fugitives, in order by these means to recall the unwary, by giving them to believe that the Christians who had remained had defeated their **adversaries**. Some of our fellow Christians hurried after us to recall us, comforting us with pleased **countenance**, and declaring that standards of the Christians, which they well knew, were raised on the wall of Jerusalem, in token that they had defeated the enemy; and they, having been thus deceived, deceived us also.*

*We ... returned confidently into the Holy City, ... many from feelings of devotion, and others in hope of obtaining and retaining possession of their inheritances, rashly and incautiously returned ...; we, however, endeavored to **dissuade** them from this altogether, fearing treachery from these **perfidious** people, and so went away from them. Not long after our departure, these perfidious Choermians came in great force and surrounded the Christians in the Holy City, making violent assaults on them daily, cutting off all means of **ingress and egress** to and from the city, and harassing them in various ways, so that, owing to these attacks, hunger and grief, they fell into despair, and all by common consent exposed themselves to the chances and risk of death by the hands of the enemy. They therefore left the city by night, and wandered about in the trackless and desert parts of the mountains till they at length came to a narrow pass, and there they fell into an **ambuscade** of the enemy, who ... attacked them with swords, arrows, stones and other weapons, **slew** and cut to pieces ... about seven thousand men and women, and caused such a massacre that the blood of those of the faith, with sorrow I say it, ran down the sides of the mountain like water. Young men and virgins they hurried off with them into captivity, and retired into the Holy City, where they cut the throats, as of sheep doomed to the slaughter, of the nuns, and aged and infirm men, who, unable to endure the toils of the journey and fight, had fled to the church of the Holy Sepulchre and to Calvary, a place **consecrated** by the blood of our Lord, thus perpetrating in His holy **sanctuary** such a crime as the eyes of men had never seen since the commencement of the world.*

Battalion: Military unit.

Standards: Flags.

Adversaries: Enemies.

Countenance: Expression, appearance.

Dissuade: Talk out of, advise against.

Perfidious: Untrustworthy.

Ingress and Egress: Entry and exit.

Ambuscade: Ambush.

Slew: Killed.

Consecrated: Made holy.

Sanctuary: Place of safety or refuge.

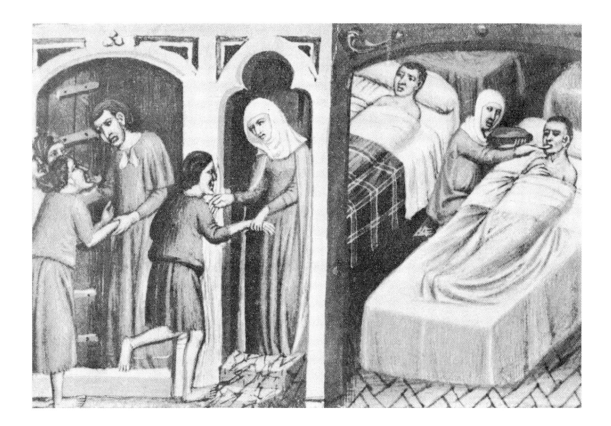

At length, as the intolerable **atrocity** of this great crime aroused the devotion of all the Christians to avenge the insult offered to their Creator, it was ... agreed that we should all ... give battle to these treacherous people. We accordingly attacked them, and fought ... till the close of the day, when darkness prevented us from distinguishing our own people from our enemies; immense numbers fell on our side; but four times as many of our adversaries were **slain**.... On the following ... day, the Knights Templars and Hospitalers ... invoked assistance from above, together with all the other religious men devoted to this war, and their forces, and the whole army of the Christians ... assembled by **proclamation** under the patriarch, and engaged in a most bloody conflict with the aforesaid Choermians and five thousand **Saracen** knights, who had recently fought under the sultan of Babylon ... ; a fierce attack was made on both sides, as we could not avoid them, for there was a powerful and numerous army on both sides of us. At length, however, we were unable to stand against such a multitude, for fresh and uninjured troops of the enemy continued to come upon us, ... and still feeling

A painting of monks and nuns welcoming travelers and caring for the sick in Jerusalem during the Crusades. Nuns, monks, the elderly, and the sick were slaughtered in the Holy City during the Seventh Crusade. © *Bettmann/Corbis. Reproduced by permission.*

Atrocity: Evil.

Slain: Killed.

Proclamation: A public order or command.

Saracen: Muslim.

the effects of the recent battle ... we were compelled to give way, abandoning to them the field, with a bloody and dearly bought victory; for great numbers more fell on their side than on ours.

And we were so assisted by **Him** who is the Saviour of souls, that not a hundred escaped by flight, but, as long as we were able to stand, we **mutually exhorted** and comforted one another in Christ, and fought so unweariedly and bravely, to the astonishment of our enemies, till we were at length taken prisoners ... or fell slain. Hence the enemy afterwards said in admiration to their prisoners: "You voluntarily threw yourselves in the way of death; why was this?" To which the prisoners replied: "We would rather die in battle, and with the death of our bodies obtain glorification for our souls than basely give way and take to flight...."

In the said battle, then, the power of the Christians was crushed, and the number of slain in both armies was **incomputable**. The masters of the Templars and Hospitalers were slain as also the masters of other orders, with their **brethren** and followers. Walter, count of Brienne, and the lord Philip de Montfort, and those who fought under the patriarch, were cut to pieces; of the Templars only eighteen escaped, and sixteen of the Hospitalers, who were afterwards sorry that they had saved themselves. Farewell.

Excerpts from "The Fall of Acre, 1291"

After having told of the glories and beauties of Acre, I will now shortly tell you of its fall and ruin, and the cause of its loss, even as I heard the tale told by right truthful men, who well remembered it. While, then, the grand doings of which I have spoken were going on in Acre, at the **instigation** of the devil there arose a violent and hateful quarrel in **Lombardy** between the **Guelfs and the Ghibellines**, which brought all evil upon the Christians. Those Lombards who dwelt at Acre took sides in this same quarrel, especially the Pisans and Genoese, both of whom had an exceedingly strong party in Acre. These men made treaties and truces with the Saracens, to the end that they might the better fight against one another within the city. When Pope Urban ... heard of this, he grieved for Christendom and for the Holy Land, and sent twelve thousand **mercenary** troops across the sea to help the Holy Land and Christendom. When these men came across the sea to Acre they did no good, but **abode** by day and by night in taverns and places of ill repute, took and **plundered** merchants and pilgrims in the public street, broke the treaty, and did much evil. Melot Sapheraph, Sultan

Him: God or Jesus Christ.

Mutually exhorted: Encouraged each other.

Incomputable: Uncountable.

Brethren: Fellow members of a religious order.

Instigation: Initiation, the act of beginning.

Lombardy: A part of Italy.

Guelfs and Ghibellines: Opposing political factions or groups in the Middle Ages that had different views about the power of the pope versus the power of the German emperor.

Mercenary: Soldier for hire.

Abode: Stayed.

Plundered: Robbed.

of Babylon, an exceedingly wise man, most potent in arms and bold in action, when he heard of this, and knew of the hateful quarrels of the people of Acre, called together his counselors and held a parliament in Babylon, wherein he complained that the truces had frequently been broken and violated, to the prejudice of himself and his people. After a debate had been held upon this matter, he gathered together a mighty **host**, and reached the city of Acre without any resistance, because of their quarrels with one another, cutting down and wasting all the vineyards and fruit trees and all the gardens and orchards, which are most lovely thereabout. When the Master of the Templars [William of Beaujeu], a very wise and brave knight, saw this, he feared that the fall of the city was at hand…. He took counsel with his brethren about how peace could be restored, and then went out to meet the Sultan, who was his own very especial friend, to ask him whether they could by any means repair the broken truce. He obtained these terms from the Sultan, **to wit**, that because of his love for the Sultan and the honor in which the Sultan held him, the broken truce might be restored by every man in Acre paying one Venetian penny. So the Master of the Templars was glad, and, departing from the Sultan, called together all the people and preached a sermon to them in the Church of St. Cross, setting forth how, by his prayers, he had **prevailed upon** the Sultan to grant that the broken treaty might be restored by a payment of one Venetian penny by each man, that **therewith** everything might be settled and quieted…. But when the people heard this, they cried out with one voice that he was the betrayer of the city, and was guilty of death. The Master, when he heard this, left the church, hardly escaped alive from the hands of the people, and took back their answer to the Sultan. When the Sultan heard this, knowing that, owing to the quarrels of the people, none of them would make any resistance, he pitched his tents, set up sixty machines, dug many mines beneath the city walls, and for forty days and nights, without any **respite**, assailed

A knight kneeling in prayer before setting out on the Seventh Crusade. Many Knights Templars and Knights Hospitallers were killed during this last Crusade. *HIP/Scala/Art Resource, NY. Reproduced by permission.*

Host: In this context, an army.

To Wit: That is to say, namely, for example.

Prevailed Upon: Persuaded.

Therewith: After that.

Respite: Rest.

the city with fire, stones, and arrows, so that [the air] seemed to be stiff with arrows.... There were at that time in the Sultan's army six hundred thousand armed, divided into three companies; so one hundred thousand continually besieged the city, and when they were weary another hundred thousand took their place before the same, two hundred thousand stood before the gates of the city ready for battle, and the duty of the remaining two hundred thousand was to supply them with everything that they needed. The gates were never closed, nor was there an hour of the day without some hard fight being fought against the Saracens by the Templars or other brethren dwelling therein. But the numbers of the Saracens grew so fast that after one hundred thousand of them had been slain two hundred thousand came back. Yet, even against all this host, they would not have lost the city had they but helped one another faithfully; but when they were fighting without the city, one party would run away and leave the other to be slain, ... and each one knew and believed his own castle and place to be so strong that he cared not for any other's castle or strong place. During this confusion the masters and brethren of the Orders alone defended themselves, and fought unceasingly against the Saracens, until they were nearly all slain; indeed, the Master and brethren of the house of the Teutonic Order, together with their followers and friends, all fell dead at one and the same time.... At last the fulfillment of their sins and the time of the fall of the city drew near; when the fortieth day of its siege was come, in the year of our Lord one thousand two hundred and ninety-two [actual date was 1291], on the twelfth day of the month of May, the most noble and glorious city of Acre, the flower, chief and pride of all the cities of the East, was taken. The people of the other cities, to wit, Jaffa, Tyre, Sidon and Ascalon, when they heard this, left all their property behind and fled to Cyprus.... We read in the stories of the loss of Acre that because of the sins of the people thereof the **four elements** fought on the side of the Saracens. First the air became so thick, dark, and cloudy that, while one castle, palace, or strong place was being stormed or burned, men could hardly see in the other castles and palaces, until their castles and palaces were attacked, and then for the first time they would have willingly defended themselves, could they have come together. Fire fought against the city, for it consumed it. Earth fought against the city, for it drank up its blood. Water also fought against the city, for it being the month of May, wherein the sea is **wont** to be very calm, when the people of Acre plainly saw that because of their sins and the darkening of the air they could not see

Four Elements: Air, fire, water, earth.

Wont: Accustomed.

The Crusades: Primary Sources

their enemies, they fled to the sea, desiring to sail to Cyprus, and whereas at first there was no wind at all at sea, of a sudden so great a storm arose that no other ship, either great or small, could come near the shore, and many who **essayed** to swim off to the ships were drowned. **Howbeit**, more than one hundred thousand men escaped to Cyprus. I have heard from a most honorable **Lord**, and from other truthful men who were present, that more than five hundred most noble ladies and maidens, the daughters of kings and princes, came down to the seashore, when the city was about to fall, carrying with them all their jewels and ornaments of gold and precious stones, of priceless value, in their bosoms, and cried aloud, whether there were any sailor there who would take all their jewels and take whichever of them he chose to wife, if only he would take them, even naked, to some safe land or island. A sailor received them all into his ship, took them across to Cyprus, with all their goods, for nothing, and went his way. But who he was, whence he came, or whither he went, no man knows to this day. Very many other noble ladies and damsels were drowned or slain. It would take long to tell what grief and **anguish** was there. While the Saracens were within the city, but before they had taken it, fighting from castle to castle, from one palace and strong place to another, so many men **perished** on either side that they walked over their corpses as it were over a bridge. When all the inner city was lost, all who still remained alive fled into the exceeding strong castle of the Templars, which was straightway **invested** on all sides by the Saracens; yet the Christians bravely defended it for two months, and before it almost all the nobles and chiefs of the Sultan's army fell dead. For when the city inside the walls was burned, yet the towers of the city, and the Templars' castle, which was in the city, remained, and with these the people of the city kept the Saracens within the city from getting out, as before they had **hindered** their coming in, until of all the Saracens who had entered the city not one remained alive, but all fell by fire or by the sword. When the Saracen nobles saw the others lying dead, and themselves unable to escape from the city, they fled for refuge into the mines which they had dug under the great tower, that they might make their way through the wall and so get out. But the Templars and others who were in the castle, seeing that they could not hurt the Saracens with stones and the like, because of the mines wherein they were, undermined the great tower of the castle, and flung it down upon the mines and the Saracens therein, and all perished alike. When the other Saracens without the city saw that they had thus, as it were, failed utterly, they

Essayed: Attempted; tried.

Howbeit: Nevertheless, in spite of that, however.

Lord: Nobleman.

Anguish: Suffering.

Perished: Died.

Invested: In this context, surrounded and attacked.

Hindered: Prevented.

Dwell: Live, inhabit.

Lamentation: Expression of sorrow or great sadness.

Bewailing: Sadly regretting.

Mourning: Expression of sorrow at someone's death.

Grandeur: Greatness.

*treacherously made a truce with the Templars and Christians on the condition that they should yield up the castle, taking all their goods with them, and should destroy it, but should rebuild the city on certain terms, and **dwell** therein in peace as heretofore. The Templars and Christians, believing this, gave up the castle and marched out of it, and came down from the city towers. When the Saracens had by this means got possession both of the castle and of the city towers, they slew all the Christians alike, and led away the captives to Babylon…. When the glorious city of Acre thus fell, all the Eastern people sung of its fall in hymns of **lamentation**, such as they are wont to sing over the tombs of their dead, **bewailing** the beauty, the grandeur, and the glory of Acre even to this day. Since that day all Christian women, whether gentle or simple, who dwell along the eastern shore [of the Mediterranean] dress in black garments of **mourning** and woe for the lost **grandeur** of Acre, even to this day.*

What happened next…

As Ludolph of Suchem noted, the fall of Acre in 1291 ended the Crusader states. The historian Hans Eberhard Mayer described the last days in *The Crusades:*

> The rest of Palestine yielded without a struggle. Tyre capitulated [surrendered] on 19 May; Sidon at the end of June although the Castle of the Sea there held out until 14 July. Beirut followed on 31 July and the two Templar fortresses, Tortosa and the Castle of the Pilgrims, were evacuated on 3 and 14 August. Deliberately and carefully the Mameluks devastated [destroyed] the whole coast in order to ensure that the Franks could never return. The political victory of the Mameluks was won at the cost of the destruction of the ancient Syro-Palestinian city civilization…. Only the ruins of palaces survived to tell of former splendour.

After leaving the shore of the eastern Mediterranean, many of the Crusaders, including the religious military orders of the Templars, Teutonic Knights, and Hospitallers, kept outposts on islands such as Cyprus and Rhodes, but 1291 ended the attempted occupation of the Holy Land by Christians.

The Sultan of Babylon

Showing all the energy of someone in the United States fighting Communism in the 1950s, the Crusaders looked at the Muslims as a stereotype, or with simplified characteristics. Thus, for the Crusaders, all their Muslim opponents in the Holy Land and in the Middle East were called "Saracens," though that word actually describes one nomadic tribe in the deserts of Arabia and Syria. So, too, did the Crusaders come up with their own term for Cairo, the major city of Egypt. They called it Babylon, and thus the leader or ruler of Egypt became the "Sultan of Babylon."

Babylon was an ancient city in the Middle East, probably the wealthiest city of its age. But that age was three thousand years before the Crusades. The word, however, still had power. It meant a place that had great wealth and luxury but also great sin and immoral behavior. So Crusaders talked about the powerful leader of the infidel, or unbeliever, as the ruler or sultan of such a place. So strong was the use of the term in the popular imagination that a romance or adventure poem was written in the fourteenth or fifteenth century called "The Sultan of Babylon," telling tall tales of the Crusades.

Others returned to their homes in Europe, and some Christian merchants managed to stay on in parts of the Middle East.

Did you know...

- The Crusades were crushed in 1291, but the idea did not die. In 1300, with a rumor that the Mongols had defeated the Mamluks, there was another call for a Crusade, but nothing came of it.

- The Knights Templars, who had defended the Holy Land for almost two centuries, did not do well after the end of the Crusades. So powerful had they become that they made enemies in Europe. The king of France managed to get them disbanded in 1312; he took their property for the state.

- Another military order, the Knights Hospitallers, survived. They found a new enemy to fight, the Ottoman Turks, who became powerful in Asia Minor in the fourteenth century.

- In 1366 the Catholic pope, Urban VI, called yet another Crusade, this time to battle the Ottoman Turks near the Black Sea. The goal, however, was not to occupy the Holy Land but to keep the Muslim Turks from invading Europe. The Christians once again were defeated.

Consider the following...

- The Crusaders managed to carve out a slice of conquered land along the eastern Mediterranean as a result of the First Crusade and to hold part of it for almost two hundred years. What changes do you think happened to the way of life of these Crusaders and their descendants who lived in this conquered territory, the Latin Kingdom, over those two centuries? How "European" were they after all those years?

- Discuss the shifting alliances between the Crusaders, the Byzantines, and the Muslims during the Crusades. Was it always a matter of the Christians against Islam?

- Discuss some of the major changes to come about in the world as a result of the Crusades.

For More Information

Books

Brundage, James, ed. *The Crusades: A Documentary History.* Milwaukee, WI: Marquette University Press, 1962.

Hindley, Geoffrey. *The Crusades: A History of Armed Pilgrimage and Holy War.* London: Constable, 2003.

Mayer, Hans Eberhard. *The Crusades.* 2nd ed. New York: Oxford University Press, 1988.

Munro, Dana C., trans. "Letters of the Crusades." *Translations and Reprints from the Original Sources of European History.* Philadelphia: University of Pennsylvania, 1896.

Web Sites

"The Crusades." *The ORB: On-line Reference Book for Medieval Studies.* http://the-orb.net/textbooks/crusade/seventhcru.html (accessed on August 4, 2004).

Fordham University. "The Capture of Jerusalem." *Internet Medieval Sourcebook.* http://www.fordham.edu/halsall/source/1144falljlem.html (accessed on August 4, 2004).

Fordham University. "The Fall of Acre, 1291." *Internet Medieval Source-book*. http://www.fordham.edu/halsall/source/1291acre.html (accessed on August 4, 2004).

Call to Arms

2

The religious wars known in the West as the Crusades had to be sold to the faithful. Such a sales job included impassioned words from various popes as well as reports of terrible wrongs done to Christian pilgrims, or travelers, in the Holy Land. Songs and poetry were also used to convince the common people and nobles alike of the need for a holy war against the followers of Islam to recapture the cities and sites in the Middle East that were sacred to Christianity. Today we would call such speeches "half-true news" and entertainment aimed at convincing people of the rightness of a cause "propaganda." At the time of the Crusades, from the end of the eleventh century to the end of the thirteenth, people in Europe had little experience with such manipulation. Most could not read or write, so they believed what their religious and civil leaders told them. Entertainment came in the form of poets and singers called troubadours. The stories and ballads spun by these aristocratic writers and performers also entered into the subconscious of simple people, forming a strong picture of the brave knights, or Christian warriors, battling the evil infidel, or Muslim.

The Muslims also had a propaganda machine through their religious leaders, historians, and poets. Busy feuding or fighting with each other, the people of the Middle East were caught unprepared to deal with the invasion of the First Crusade in 1096. The divisions in the world of Islam created by competing branches of the religion and rival dynasties, or ruling lines, allowed the Crusaders to take the Holy Land and set up their Crusader states in Palestine, a strip of land along the eastern Mediterranean from Jerusalem in the south to Antioch in the north. Such divisions were soon put aside, however, as strong leaders from the twelfth and thirteenth centuries, such as Zengi, Nur al-Din (also called Nureddin), Saladin, and Baybars rallied the Muslims around the idea of *jihad,* or holy war, against the infidel. (It is worth noting that both the Christians and the Muslims called followers of the other religion "infidels," or unbelievers.) Hand in hand with such leaders, the poets, writers, and chroniclers (historians) of the time began to pour out warnings to the people of the Middle East to put aside their differences and fight the common enemy, Christian invaders.

Not everyone, everywhere was caught up in this crusading craze, however. Some resisted the call to arms and tried to examine the real motives for such a holy war. These voices were few. On both sides most were willing to put their lives on the line for such a cause. In Europe there were plenty of knights and noblemen who were looking for opportunities in a new land. The pope's promise of wiping away all their sins if they went on Crusade also attracted many soldiers who had committed numerous sins in their pasts. For the believers in Islam, the idea of becoming a soldier of God (or Allah, as they called him) was part of the religion. Muslims have a duty to fight for their religion, though they cannot be forced to fight. Still, from the Muslim point of view their lands were being invaded, and few resisted the call to arms to fight the Christian invader.

The call to arms for the Crusades lasted more than two centuries and came from a variety of sources. The first section of this chapter, "*Deus Volt*—God Wills It!," examines the role of the leader of the Christian Church, the pope, in calling for a Crusade, in the excerpt "Urban II: Speech at the Council of Clermont, 1095." The importance of the call for help from Christians in the Holy Land is also highlighted in

"The Decline of Christian Power in the Holy Land, 1164: Letter from Aymeric, Patriarch of Antioch, to Louis VII of France." The second section, "Poetry of the Crusades," looks at the importance of literature in promoting the Crusades, with an excerpt from the medieval French epic poem, *The Song of Roland* and a troubadour song from Conon de Béthune, "Ahi! Amours! Com dure departie" ("Alas, Love, What Hard Leave"). The Muslim perspective or point of view is presented in the third section, "The Muslim Call to Arms," in a poem on the Crusades from the Islamic poet Abu l-Musaffar al-Abiwardi, as collected in "The Perfect History" from the medieval Muslim historian Ibn al-Athir. A further look at the divided nature of the Islamic world comes in an excerpt from *The Book of the Maghrib* by the Muslim chronicler Ibn Said. The fourth and final section, "Anti-Crusades," offers another viewpoint in an excerpt from the "*Annales Herbipolenses,*" written by an anonymous German historian critical of the Second Crusade (1147–49).

Deus Volt—God Wills It!

Excerpt from "Urban II: Speech at the Council of Clermont 1095."

Speech given by Pope Urban II; Reprinted in *Source Book for Medieval History*; Edited by Oliver J. Thatcher and Edgar Holmes McNeal; Published in 1905

Excerpt from "The Decline of Christian Power in the Holy Land, 1164: Letter from Aymeric, Patriarch of Antioch to Louis VII of France" (1164)

Originally written by Aymeric, Patriarch of Antioch; Reprinted in "Letters of the Crusaders," from *Translations and Reprints from the Original Sources of European History*; Edited by Dana C. Munro; Published in 1896

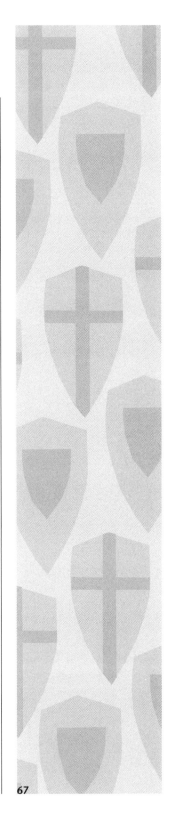

It is important to remember that the Crusades got their start by the written and spoken word. The emperor of the Byzantine Empire in the late eleventh century, Alexius I, wrote to the pope in Rome asking for help against the threat of a new Muslim power in Asia Minor, the Seljuk Turks. Pope Urban II then spoke forcefully to church leaders and to the nobles of Europe on several occasions, in favor of a holy war to the Middle East. In return for going on such a Crusade, the soldiers of Christ would be forgiven their past sins. This was a strong encouragement to the knights of Europe. Urban II also told of atrocities, or cruel acts, supposedly committed against the Christians of the Holy Land by the Muslims. His speech at the Council of Clermont in 1095 was particularly influential in gaining public support for a holy war of Christianity against Islam known as the First Crusade (1095–99). Of course, Urban II was only one of many church leaders to call for Crusades. Later came the works of Saint Bernard of Clairvaux, who preached the Second Crusade (1147–49), and Pope Innocent III, who preached the Fourth Crusade (1202–04), among others.

Pope Urban II calling the First Crusade at the Council of Clermont in 1095.
© *Archivo Iconografico, S.A./ Corbis. Reproduced by permission.*

There were numerous calls for help from the Holy Land in addition to the first letter from Alexius I of the Byzantine Empire. The patriarch of Antioch, or leader of the Eastern Orthodox Church in that city, wrote to the king of France, Louis VII, in 1164 to complain of the weakened power of the Crusader states that were created after the victorious First Crusade. Aymeric, the patriarch of Antioch, explains in his letter the political and military situation in the

Crusader states almost twenty years after the failure of the Second Crusade. The Crusaders were battling a new force in the region, the Muslim military leader Nur al-Din, who had conquered all of Syria and was then moving into Egypt to bring that rich state into his growing empire. The Crusader states, especially the Kingdom of Jerusalem, had their eyes on Egypt as well, not only for its natural resources but also to avoid being caught with strong enemies completely surrounding them. The defeat of Crusader armies in 1164 by Nur al-Din and his general Shirkuh had further weakened the Christian position in the Holy Land, and Aymeric was appealing to Louis VII, one of the leaders of the failed Second Crusade, in the hope of receiving aid from the West. Such aid, in the form of the Third Crusade (1189–92), would have to wait until after the disastrous fall of Jerusalem in 1187 to the new Muslim military leader, Saladin.

Things to Remember While Reading Excerpts about the Christian Call for a Crusade:

- Speeches and documents produced by church leaders, such as the pope, were heard and read by a small minority of the people of Europe. The message of the Crusade was spread to the common people by local preachers, such as Peter the Hermit, a wandering preacher who attracted thousands to his outdoor meetings.

- Peter the Hermit was, in a way, too successful with his preaching, for he inspired the "People's Crusade," which took off from Europe for the Holy Land for the First Crusade before the regular armies set sail. These untrained forces, which included entire families, were filled with a desire to do God's will, and to escape several seasons of poor harvests in Europe. At least twenty thousand joined Peter's forces, and most were killed either on their way to Constantinople, where the First Crusade was gathering, or just outside Constantinople, where the Turks cut down this untrained crowd.

- The tales of atrocities committed against Christians in the Holy Land also inspired other Crusaders, such as the German leaders Emich of Leiningen and Volkmar, to begin their Crusade closer to home, killing Jews throughout Germany.

- The First Crusade was the only successful Crusade for the Christians. They captured Jerusalem and were able to establish a Christian foothold along the shore of the eastern Mediterranean with four Crusader states, the Kingdom of Jerusalem, the Principality of Antioch, and the Counties of Tripoli and Edessa, that created a Crusader presence in the Middle East for the next two centuries.

- The Crusader states in the Holy Land were completely surrounded by unfriendly Muslims. The Christians were able to survive by a mixture of military might and smart dealings with competing Muslims groups. They took advantage of the divided Islamic world of the twelfth century by making treaties with, for example, the ruling dynasty in Egypt, the Fatimids, against the Syrian Muslims led by the Turkish Zangid line.

- No treaties could save the Crusader states, though, when the Muslims began uniting under strong leaders, such as Zengi and his son, Nur al-Din. These Turkish Muslims took the Crusader state of Edessa in 1144, an action that spurred the Second Crusade. But with the defeat of that Crusade, it was clear that the balance of power had shifted in the Middle East. The Crusader states were in need of more and more support from Europe, support that was not always available.

Excerpt from "Urban II: Speech at the Council of Clermont, 1095"

*Most beloved **brethren**: Urged by necessity, I, Urban, by the permission of God chief bishop and **prelate** over the whole world, have come into these parts as an ambassador with a divine **admonition** to you, the servants of God.... Although, O sons of God, you have promised more firmly than ever to keep the peace among yourselves and to preserve the rights of the church, there remains still an important work for you to do. Freshly **quickened** by the di-*

Brethren: Fellow members of a religious order.

Prelate: High officer of the church.

Admonition: Strong warning or criticism.

Quickened: Enlivened, stimulated, encouraged.

vine correction, you must apply the strength of your righteousness to another matter which concerns you as well as God. For your brethren who live in the east are in urgent need of your help, and you must **hasten** to give them the aid which has often been promised them. For, as the most of you have heard, the Turks and Arabs have attacked them and have conquered the territory of Romania [the Greek empire] as far west as the shore of the Mediterranean and the Hellespont, which is called the Arm of St. George. They have occupied more and more of the lands of those Christians, and have overcome them in seven battles. They have killed and captured many, and have destroyed the churches and devastated the empire. If you permit them to continue thus for awhile with impurity, the faithful of God will be much more widely attacked by them. On this account I, or rather the Lord, **beseech** you as Christ's **heralds,** to publish this everywhere and to persuade all people of whatever rank, foot-soldiers and knights, poor and rich, to carry aid promptly to those Christians and to destroy that vile race from the lands of our friends. I say this to those who are present, it is meant also for those who are absent. Moreover, Christ commands it.

All who die by the way, whether by land or by sea, or in battle against the **pagans,** shall have immediate **remission** of sins. This I grant them through the power of God with which I am **invested.** O what a disgrace if such a despised and base race, which worships demons, should conquer a people which has the faith of **omnipotent** God and is made glorious with the name of Christ! With what **reproaches** will the Lord overwhelm us if you do not aid those who, with us, **profess** the Christian religion! Let those who have been accustomed unjustly to wage private warfare against the faithful now go against the **infidels** and end with victory this war which should have been begun long ago. Let those who for a long time have been robbers now become knights. Let those who have been fighting against their brothers and relatives now fight in a proper way against the barbarians. Let those who have been serving as **mercenaries** for small pay now obtain the eternal reward. Let those who have been wearing themselves out in both body and soul now work for a double honor. Behold! on this side will be the sorrowful and poor, on that, the rich; on this side, the enemies of the Lord, on that, his friends. Let those who go not put off the journey, but rent their lands and collect money for their expenses; and as soon as winter is over and spring comes, let them eagerly set out on the way with God as their guide.

Hasten: Hurry.

Beseech: To ask someone desperately for something.

Heralds: Messengers, champions.

Pagans: Those who do not believe in the Christian God.

Remission: Cancellation.

Invested: Empowered.

Omnipotent: All-knowing, all-powerful.

Reproaches: Scoldings, criticisms.

Profess: Accept.

Infidels: Unbelievers.

Mercenaries: Soldiers of fortune, soldiers hired to fight.

Pilgrims arriving in the Holy Land in response to Pope Urban II's call for the First Crusade. © *Bettmann/Corbis. Reproduced by permission.*

Patriarch: A church leader in the Eastern Orthodox faith.

Apostolic See: One of the major religious districts of the Eastern Orthodox Church.

Benediction: Blessing.

Excerpt from "The Decline of Christian Power in the Holy Land, 1164: Letter from Aymeric, Patriarch of Antioch to Louis VII of France"

*Aymeric, by the grace of God, **patriarch** of the holy **Apostolic See** of Antioch, to Louis, illustrious king of the French,—greeting and Apostolic **benediction**.*

*It would be fitting that we should always write joyful **tidings** to his royal majesty and should increase the splendor of his heart by the splendor and delight of our words. But the reverse has ever been our lot. The causes for tears, **forsooth**, are constant, the grief and the groaning are continuous, and we are unable to speak except of what concerns us. For the proverb says: "Where the grief is, there is also the tongue and hand." The deaths of the Christians are frequent and the captures which we see daily. Moreover, the wasting away of the church in the East **afflicts** with **ineradicable** grief us who, tortured internally even to our destruction, are dying while living in anguish of soul, and, leading a life more bitter than death, as a culmination of our miseries, are wholly unable to die. Nor is there anyone who turns his heart towards us and out of pity directs his hand to aid us. But not to protract our words, the few Christians who are here cry out to you, together with us, and implore your **clemency**, which with God's assistance is sufficient to liberate us and the church of God in the East.*

*And now we will tell you of all the events which have happened to us. In the **Lent** which has just passed, a certain one [Nureddin] of the men who are about us, who is held as chief among the **Saracens**, and who oppresses our Christian population far more than all who have gone before, and the leader of his army [Schirkuh], having gotten possession of Damascus, the latter entered Egypt with a great force of Turks, in order to conquer the country. Accordingly, the king of Egypt, who is also called the sultan of Babylon, distrusting his own **valor** and that of his men, held a most warlike council to determine how to meet the advancing Turks and how he could obtain the aid of the king of Jerusalem. For he wisely preferred to rule under **tribute** rather than to be deprived of both life and kingdom.*

*The former, therefore ... entered Egypt, and favored by certain men of that land, captured and fortified a certain city. In the meantime the sultan made an alliance with the lord king [Amalric] by promising to pay tribute each year and release all the Christian captives in Egypt, and obtained the aid of the lord king. The latter before setting out, committed the care of his kingdom and land, until his return, to us and to our new prince, his **kinsman** Bohemond, son of the former prince, Raymond.*

*Therefore, the great **devastator** of the Christian people, ... collected together from all sides the kings and races of the infidels and offered a peace and truce to our prince.... His reason was that he wished to **traverse** our land with greater freedom in order to devas-*

Tidings: News, information.

Forsooth: Indeed.

Afflicts: Causes pain.

Ineradicable: Unable to be removed.

Clemency: Mercy.

Lent: A time of fasting and penitence observed by Christians during the forty weekdays before Easter.

Saracens: Muslims.

Valor: Courage.

Tribute: Periodic payment from one state to another.

Kinsman: Relative.

Devastator: Destroyer.

Traverse: To cross, pass through.

tate the kingdom of Jerusalem and to be able to bear aid to his **vassal** fighting in Egypt. But our prince was unwilling to make peace with him until the return of our lord king.

When the former saw that he was not able to accomplish what he had proposed, full of **wrath**, he turned his weapons against us and laid siege to a certain fortress of ours, called Harrenc, twelve miles distant from our city. But those who were besieged—7000 in number including warriors, men and women—cried loudly to us, ceasing neither day nor night, to have pity on them, and fixed a day beyond which it would be impossible for them to hold out. Our prince having collected all his forces, set out from Antioch on the day of St. Lawrence and proceeded as far as the fortress in entire safety. For the Turks in their cunning gave up the siege and withdrew a short distance from the fortress to some narrow passes in their own country.

On the next day our men followed the enemy to that place and while they were marching … battle was engaged and they fled. The conflict was so disastrous that hardly anyone of ours of any rank escaped, except a few whom the strength of their horses or some lucky chance rescued from the **tumult**. Those captured were our prince [Bohemond III], the count of Tripoli [Raymond II], … and some of the brethren of the **Templars and Hospitalers** who had come from the county of Tripoli with the count. Of the people, some were killed, others captured; very few escaped; men, horses and weapons were almost entirely destroyed.

After the slaughter of the Christians the Turks returned to the … fortress, captured it, and by compact **conducted** the feeble multitude of women, children and wounded as far as Antioch. Afterwards they advanced to the City, devastated the whole country as far as the sea with fire and sword and exercised their tyranny according to their **lusts** on everything which met their eyes.

God is witness that the **remnant** which is left us is in no way sufficient to guard the walls night and day, and owing to the scarcity of men, we are **obliged** to entrust their safety and defense to some whom we suspect. Neglecting the church services, the clergy and **presbyters** guard the gates. We ourselves are looking after the defense of the walls and, as far as possible, are repairing, with great and unremitting labor, the many portions which have been broken down by earthquakes. And all this in vain, unless God shall look upon us with a more kindly **countenance**. For we do not hope to

Vassal: Underling, assistant.

Wrath: Anger.

Tumult: Commotion.

Templars and Hospitalers: Two military religious orders.

Conducted: Escorted.

Lusts: Intense longings.

Remnant: Remains, or that which is left over.

Obliged: Forced.

Presbyters: Elders, or senior officials, of the church.

Countenance: Support or approval.

*hold out longer, **inasmuch as** the valor of the men of the present day has been exhausted and is of no avail....*

Above all, the only anchor which is left in this extremity for our hope is in you. Because we have heard from everybody of your greatness, because we have understood that you, more than all the other kings of the West, always have the East in mind.... And it is our hope that by your hand the Lord will visit His people and will have compassion on us.

*May the sighings and groanings of the Christians enter the ear of the most high and incomparable prince; may the tortures and griefs of the captives strike his heart. And, not to make our letter too long, **lest** we should waste away in this vain hope and be for a long time consumed by the shadow of death, may his royal majesty **deign** to write to us and tell us his pleasure. Whatever we undergo by his command will not be difficult for us. May our Lord Jesus Christ increase in the heart of the king the desire which we desire, and may He in whose hand are the hearts of kings **enkindle** that heart! Amen.*

Inasmuch As: Considering that.

Lest: To avoid the risk that.

Deign: Do something beneath one's dignity or office.

Enkindle: To set on fire or into action.

What happened next...

The papacy, or office of the pope, continued to promote Crusades throughout the twelfth century and into the thirteenth. With the Second Crusade and Third Crusade, the church was a strong supporter of the Christian warriors. In the beginning of the thirteenth century Pope Innocent III, asked for another holy war against the Muslims in the Holy Land. But the Fourth Crusade (1202–04) was one of the great tragedies for the Crusader movement. Proclaimed and blessed by Innocent III, that Crusade never went to the Holy Land but instead attacked the Christian city of Zara on the Yugoslavian coast and then moved on and sacked the capital of the Byzantine Empire, Constantinople, another Christian city, though part of the Eastern Orthodox faith. Innocent excommunicated, or expelled, the disobedient Crusaders, but he later had to accept the fact of this invasion and actually used the victory in Constantinople as an excuse to try to spread the western, or Latin, church rites and traditions over

The Speech That Launched the Holy Wars

What exactly Pope Urban II said at the Council of Clermont is not known, not because there were no reports of it, but because there were too many. In fact, five different chroniclers give five somewhat different versions of that speech. But it is clear that the pope produced arguments for a Crusade that he thought would have the widest possible appeal. In those days before polls, Urban II had to have his finger on the pulse of those he was counting on: the nobles and knights of Europe. Naturally, part of that message was an emphasis on the threat to Christianity that the Turks, recent converts to the faith of Islam, presented.

Perhaps more important, however, was the pope's offer of an indulgence, or the offer to get rid of a person's sins. Normally, Catholics had to confess their sins to a priest and then receive duties, or penance, to perform as a way to absolve, or relieve, them of such bad deeds. But Urban II announced at Clermont that anyone who joined the Crusade for religious reasons would be freed from such penance. Although historians argue whether this was a complete forgiveness of all sins, it is clear that most Crusaders thought that it was. The pope's offer was actually only one of remission, or cancellation, of any earthly duties of penance for Crusaders. Once, however, the message of the Crusade was preached on the local level, this promise was extended to the cancellation of such sins in heaven as well as on Earth. So popular was it with the participants that this idea of an indulgence was used in each of the Crusades promoted by the church.

the "Latin Empire of Constantinople" that the Crusaders had formed. But these efforts failed, and the schism, or separation, of East and West was only made worse. Such church-sponsored Crusades came to an end with the Sixth Crusade, which the German emperor Frederick II mounted without much religious sponsorship. The need for church propaganda was taken out of the Crusader movement, replaced with the more material concerns of expansion of empire. And for this, a professional army was needed.

Did you know...

- Officially, the pope was the only one with the proper authority to call a Crusade, but many small expeditions and several full Crusades were proclaimed by people who were not church officials, such as the German emperor Frederick II at the Sixth Crusade (1228–29). By that time the idea of a Crusade had become one more area of competition between the pope and secular, or nonreligious, rulers.

- As the Crusades proceeded, the papacy became more professional in spreading the word to the faithful. No bull (official pronouncement) was made for the First Crusade. Instead, it was left to local preachers to talk up the movement. By the Second Crusade matters had become more authoritative, with an official letter from the pope explaining the need for the Crusade and listing the privileges of the Crusaders. These privileges included, besides the indulgence, a guarantee to protect the lands of the Crusaders while they were away fighting and sometimes even a cancellation of bad debts, or money owed but not yet paid back. By 1181 the preparations for Crusades had become formalized in the papal bull known as *Cor nostrum,* which was published in all churches and announced by the priests.

- In 1198, in preparation for the Fourth Crusade, a general executive office was set up by the pope for the "business of the cross," as it was described at the time. Freelance preachers had also come into the business by this time, roaming the countryside and preaching the Crusade.

- By the thirteenth century the church had established a system to spread the word of a Crusade to every corner of the West.

Consider the following...

- What appeals and information did Pope Urban II use to persuade the faithful to go on the First Crusade? Were these emotional or rational arguments, or were they a mixture of both?

- The propaganda for the First Crusade came both in the written word and in the spoken word. Give examples of both types.

- Discuss some of the ways in which the Catholic Church spread the word of the Crusades.

For More Information

Books

Mayer, Hans Eberhard. *The Crusades.* 2nd ed. New York: Oxford University Press, 1988.

Munro, Dana C., ed. "Letters of the Crusaders." *Translations and Reprints from the Original Sources of European History.* Philadelphia: University of Pennsylvania, 1896.

Riley-Smith, Jonathan, ed. *The Oxford Illustrated History of the Crusades.* New York: Oxford University Press, 1995.

Thatcher, Oliver J., and Edgar Holmes McNeal, eds. *A Source Book for Medieval History.* New York: Scribners, 1905.

Web Sites

Fordham University. "The Decline of Christian Power in the Holy Land, 1164: Letter from Aymeric, Patriarch of Antioch to Louis VII of France." *Internet Medieval Sourcebook.* http://www.fordham.edu/halsall/source/aymeric1164.html (accessed on August 4, 2004).

Fordham University. "Urban II: Speech at Council of Clermont, 1095, According to Fulcher of Chartres." *Internet Medieval Sourcebook.* http://www.fordham.edu/halsall/source/urban2-5vers.html (accessed on August 4, 2004).

Poetry of the Crusades

Excerpt from The Song of Roland *(c. 1100)*
**Originally written by Anonymous;
Translated by Dorothy L. Sayers; Published in 1957**

*Excerpt from "Ahi! Amours! Com dure departie/Alas, Love,
What Hard Leave," (1219)*
**Originally written by Conon de Béthune;
Reprinted in *Lyrics of the Troubadours and Trouvères*; Edited by
Frederick Goldin; Published in 1973**

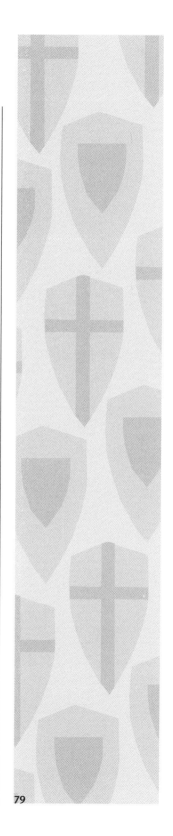

Literature also helped promote the Crusades. However, with so many people unable to read in the Middle Ages, such literature serving the needs of propaganda had to be able to reach more than simply the small educated class. Much of medieval literature was made up of chronicles, or histories, kept by clerks of the church and written in Latin. These histories were not accessible enough or easy enough to understand to be used to promote the Crusades. Instead, more popular entertainment, such as songs and long poems, had the power to move the people, for they were not only written but also performed by traveling singers and poets and by court musicians called minstrels.

One early form of literature about the Crusades was provided in long epic poems that became popular in the twelfth century. Such poems of heroic deeds were fashionable in France and Germany. In France they were called *chansons de geste,* meaning "songs of great or heroic actions." The most famous of these chansons is *The Song of Roland,* written between about 1098 and 1100 by an unknown poet or poets. This poem tells of an actual historical event involving the famous soldier-king Charlemagne, who was coming back from a military campaign in Spain in 778. Those protecting the last of the long line of Charlemagne's soldiers were killed in an ambush, slaughtered in the Roncesvalles (or in old French, Rencesvals) pass of the Pyrenees mountains by Basques, the natives of a portion of northern Spain. The poem, however, changes this enemy to Muslims, also called Saracens or Paynims.

A tale of betrayal and loyalty, *The Song of Roland* features the heroic knight Roland and his friend Oliver, who die, along with their fellow soldiers, as they protect the king's rearguard. Ganelon, Roland's stepfather, turns traitor to the Muslim leader Marsile and brings about the death of these French knights. Attacked, the courageous Roland refuses to blow his battle horn for help and thus bring the king back into an ambush. Finally, though, after fighting bravely and as he is about to die, Roland blows his horn powerfully, and the king comes too late to help but not too late to avenge Roland's death. The scenes excerpted here recount the battle, while the rest of the poem finds the king getting back at the Muslims and at Ganelon for this sad deed, finally conquering all of Muslim Spain and forcing the infidels, or non-believers, to convert to Christianity.

Thus, in the poem, Charlemagne becomes the great protector in Europe against the invasion of Islam. In fact, Muslim Spain was one of the most powerful and cultured lands in the eighth century, at a time when the Christian powers of Europe were still unorganized, and it remained so into the time of the Crusades. The conquest of Spain as represented in *The Song of Roland* is a long way from the historical truth. Yet at the time the poem was written the preparation for and events of the First Crusade (1095–99) were fresh in the minds of Europeans. Although the events of *The Song of Roland* took place several hundred years before the Crusades, the topic of Christians fighting against Muslims, or Saracens, was the same one that church leaders were preaching to the faithful at the end of the eleventh century. Many scholars therefore consider *The Song of Roland* to be an early form of propaganda to incite and encourage Christians to answer the call to arms against the Muslims in the Holy Land. Throughout the long poem, Muslims, or Saracens, are shown to be evil monsters. This was the picture Pope Urban II hoped to paint of the enemy when he spoke in favor of a Crusade.

Songs also played a part in selling the Crusader message. These became part of the troubadour tradition, the aristocratic or noble poets, singers, and musicians of southern France, who wrote from the eleventh to the thirteenth centuries. They wrote in praise of love and great loss and were often veterans of the Crusades, spinning tales of battles against the Saracens. Their writings frequently were performed by lower-class entertainers known as *jongleurs,* who sang and played musical instruments and sometimes even helped compose the poems and songs. Written in the dialect of southern France, the favorite themes of such songs were love, war, and nature. Northern France later developed a similar tradition. There the troubadours were known as *trouvères.* In the German tradition they were known as *Minnesängers.*

A portrait of Roland from *The Song of Roland.* **Many scholars consider this epic an early form of propaganda to incite and encourage Christians to answer the call to arms against the Muslims in the Holy Land.** *© Bettmann/Corbis. Reproduced by permission.*

Conon de Béthune (1160–1219) was one of many powerful nobles who took up the troubadour tradition, and as with many other troubadours and *trouvères,* he was an important Crusader. He took part in the Third Crusade (1189–92) as well as the Fourth Crusade (1202–04). He distinguished himself during the Fourth Crusade and stayed on in the new Crusader state created in Constantinople by the Byzantine Empire. He was known for an intense strength and a military spirit that sets his work apart from other such poets. The excerpt provided here is one of his best-known poems and blends the themes of love, loss, and war in one call to arms.

Things to Remember While Reading Excerpts about Crusader Poetry:

- *The Song of Roland* consists of about four thousand lines of poetry or verse. These lines are further divided into almost three hundred units of irregular length called *laisses*. Each line has about ten syllables and ends with a sound similar to that of the previous line, but it does not necessarily exactly rhyme with the preceding line.

- *Chansons de geste,* such as *The Song of Roland,* were meant to be performed, accompanied with music, for special social gatherings.

- The poems and songs of the troubadours were written in old Provençal, a dialect of southern France, while the *trouvères* poems were written in old French.

- The poems of the troubadour and *trouvères* traditions did not have a typical or patterned rhyme scheme or structure. Novelty and creativity were the most important elements in their form.

- Such poems usually consisted of three to ten stanzas, or poetical paragraphs, and then usually ended with an *envoy,* a verbal send-off of some sort, saying good-bye and wishing to be remembered.

Excerpts from The Song of Roland

81

Oliver's climbed a hill above the plain,

Whence he can look on all the land of Spain,

And see how vast the **Saracen array;**

All those bright helms with gold and jewels gay,

And all those shields, those coats of **burnished mail;**

And all those lances from which the **pennons** wave;

Even their squadrons defy all estimate,

He cannot count them, their numbers are so great;

Stout as he is, he's mightily dismayed.

He hastens down as swiftly as he may,

Comes to the French and tells them all his tale.

Whence: From where.

Saracen: Muslim.

Array: Gather.

Burnished: Polished.

Mail: Armor.

Pennons: Flags.

Stout: In this context, strong.

Quoth Oliver: "The **Paynim** *strength I've seen;*

Never on earth has such a hosting been:

A hundred thousand in **van** *ride under shield*

Their helmets laced, their **hauberks** *all agleam*

Their spears upright, with heads of shining steel.

You'll have such battle as **ne'er** *was fought on field.*

My lords of France, God give you strength at need!

Save you stand fast, this field we cannot keep."

The French all say, "Foul shame it were to flee!

We're yours till death; no man of us will yield." …

85

"Companion Roland, your **Olifant** *now blow;*

Charles in the passes will hear it as he goes,

Trust me, the French will all return right so."

"Now God forbid," Roland makes answer wroth,

"That living man should say he saw me go

Blowing of horns for any Paynim foe!

Ne'er shall my **kindred** *be put to such* **reproach**.

When I shall stand in this great clash of **hosts**

I'll strike a thousand and then sev'n hundred strokes,

Blood-red the steel of **Durendal** *shall flow.*

Stout are the French, they will do battle bold,

These men of Spain shall die and have no hope." …

88

When Roland sees that battle there must be

Leopard nor lion ne'er grew so fierce as he.

He calls the French, bids Oliver give heed:

"Sir friend and comrade, such words you shall not
speak!

When the King gave us the French to serve this need

Quoth: Said.

Paynim: Heathen or Muslim.

Van: Vanguard; the troops moving at the front of an army.

Hauberks: A long protective shirt or armor.

Ne'er: Never.

Olifant: Roland's horn.

Kindred: Relatives.

Reproach: Strong disapproval.

Hosts: Armies.

Durendal: Roland's unbreakable sword.

These twenty thousand he chose to do the deed;

*And well he knew not one would **flinch** or flee.*

*Men must endure much hardship for their **liege**,*

And bear for him great cold and burning heat,

Suffer sharp wounds and let their bodies bleed.

***Smite** with your lance and I with my good steel,*

My Durendal the emperor gave to me:

And if I die, who gets it may agree

That he who bore it, a right good knight was he." …

90

The French rise up and on their feet stand close;

*All of their sins are **shriven** and made whole,*

*And the **Archbishop** God's blessing has **bestowed**.*

*Then on swift **steeds** they leap to saddlebow.*

Armed with the arms prescribed by knightly code;

All are now ready into the field to go.

Count Roland said to Oliver right so:

"Sir my companion, too true the word you spoke,

That all of us by Ganelon were sold.

He's ta'en his wage of wealth and goods and gold.

The Emperor's vengeance I think will not be slow!

Marsile the King has bargained for our bones:

He'll need the sword to fetch his purchase home." …

95

From a far land he came, from Barbary;

The Saracens he calls, and thus he speaks:

"Well are we placed this field of arms to keep;

For of these Franks the number is but weak,

And we may well despise the few we see.

Charles cannot come to help them in their need,

Flinch: Jerk from fear.

Liege: Lord or superior.

Smite: Strike.

Shriven: Absolved, gotten rid of.

Archbishop: Archbishop Turin, one of the main characters in *The Song of Roland,* a warrior and priest.

Bestowed: Been placed.

Steeds: Horses.

This is the day their deaths are all **decreed**!"

Archbishop Turpin has listened to his speech,

And hates him worse than any man that breathes.

His golden spurs he strikes into his steed,

And rides against him, right **valiant** for the deed.

He breaks the **buckler**, he's split the hauberk's steel.

Into his breast driven the lance-head deep,

He spits him through, on high his body heaves,

And hurls him dead a spear's length o'er the **lea**....

98

Samson the Duke on the Almanzor runs:

Through gilded shield and painted flowers he thrusts;

Not for defence avails the hauberk tough,

He splits his heart, his liver, and his lung,

And strikes him dead, weep any or weep none.

Cries the Archbishop: "This **feat** was knightly done!" ...

100

And **Engelier** the Gascon of Bordeaux

Spurs his good steed, slacks rein and lets him go;

With Escrimiz, Valterna's lord, he's closed,

Off from his neck the splintered buckler broke.

The hauberk's **ventail** he's shattered with the stroke.

He splits his throat between the collar-bones,

A full spear's length dead from the saddle throws;

Then says to him, "The devil take **thy** soul...."

110

Fierce is the battle and wondrous grim the fight.

Both Oliver and Roland boldly **smite**,

Thousands of strokes the stout Archbishop strikes,

The whole Twelve Peers are not a whit [a bit] behind,

And the French ranks lay on with all their might.

Decreed: Officially announced.

Valiant: Heroic.

Buckler: A round shield.

Lea: Meadow.

Samson: One of the twelve peers, or knights, who fight along with Roland and Oliver.

Feat: Accomplishment.

Engelier: Another of the twelve peers.

Ventail: A flap of mail or armor protecting the lower face during battle.

Thy: Your.

Smite: To kill by a heavy blow.

la grede France herberuerēt enui   Que africani tei mutcapmer

An illustration of an army pitching camp from *The Song of Roland.* *By permission of The British Library (Lansdowne 782).*

Heaped by the hundred thousands of Paynims lie,

None can escape unless he turns and flies,

Will he or nill [unwillingly] he, there must he leave his life.

There France must lose the noblest of her knights,

They'll see no more their kindred and their **sires**,

Nor Charles, who scans the pass with anxious eyes.

Throughout all France terrific **tempests** rise,

Thunder is heard, the stormy winds blow high,

Unmeasured rain and hail fall from the sky,

While thick and fast flashes the **levin** bright.

And true it is the earth quakes far and wide.

Far as from Saintes to Michael-of-the-Tide,

From Besançon to Wissant Port, you'd find

There's not a house but the walls crack and **rive**.

Right at high noon a darkness falls like night,

Save for the lightning there's not a gleam of light;

None that **beholds** it but is dismayed for fright,

And many say: "This is the latter time,

The world is ending, and the Great **Doom** is **nigh**."

They speak not true, they cannot read the signs:

'Tis Roland's death calls forth this mighty cry....

115

Now can the French count up the Paynim might

They see it filling the plains from side to side.

They urge on Roland and Oliver likewise

And the Twelve Peers to flee for all their lives;

To whom straightway the **Prelate** speaks his mind:

"Barons, my lords, these shameful thoughts put by;

By God I charge you, hold fast and do not fly,

Lest brave men sing ill songs in your despite.

Better it were to perish in the fight.

Soon, very soon we all are marked to die,

None of us here will see tomorrow's light;

One thing there is I promise you outright:

To you stand open the gates of Paradise,

There with the holy sweet Innocents to **bide**...."

Sires: Fathers.

Tempests: Storms.

Levin: Lightning.

Rive: Tear apart.

Beholds: Sees.

Doom: Terrible fate.

Nigh: Near.

Prelate: Church officer, in this case, Archbishop Turin.

Bide: To stay with.

126

Wondrous the battle, and it grows faster yet;

*The French fight on with rage and fury **fell**,*

*They **lop off** wrists, **hew** ribs and spines to shreds,*

*They **cleave** the harness through to the living flesh;*

On the green ground the blood runs clear and red.

[The Paynims say,] "We cannot stand the stress,

*French Fatherland, be cursed of **Mahomet**!*

Your sons are bravest of all the sons of men."

There's none of them but cries "Marsile to help!

*Ride, ride, O King, for we are hard **bested**...."*

135

Count Roland's mouth with running blood is red;

*He's burst **asunder** the temples of his head;*

He sounds his horn in anguish and distress.

King Carlon hears, and so do all the French.

Then said the King: "This horn is long of breath."

*"'Tis blown," quoth Naimon, "with all a brave
    man's strength.*

Battle there is, and that I know full well.

He that would stay you is but a traitor fell.

To arms! let sound your battle-cry to heav'n!

Make haste to bring your gallant household help!

You hear how Roland makes desperate lament!"

136

Straightway to horse the warrior lords have got;

Swift through the passes they spur and never stop.

Each unto other they speak and make response:

*"Might we reach Roland **ere** he were dead and gone,*

*We'd strike good strokes beside him in the **throng**."*

What use is that? They have delayed too long....

Fell: Fierce, cruel.

Lop Off: Cut or chop off.

Hew: Chop.

Cleave: Cut, split.

Mahomet: Muhammad, the founder of Islam.

Bested: Defeated.

Asunder: Into pieces.

Ere: Before.

Throng: Crowd.

160

The Paynims say, "Why were we ever born?

Woe worth the while! our day of doom has dawned.

Now have we lost our **peerage** and our lords,

The mighty Carlon comes on with all his force,

Of those of France we hear the shrilling horns.

The cry 'Mountjoy' sounds fearfully abroad.

So grim of mood is Roland in his **wrath**

No man alive can put him to the sword.

Let fly at him, and then give up the war."

So they let fly; spears, lances they outpour,

Darts and **jereeds** and feathered shafts galore.

The shield of Roland is pierced and split and **scored**,

The mail rings riven, and all his hauberk torn,

Yet in his body he is not touched at all.

Though under him, with thirty wounds and more,

His **Veillantif** is stricken dead and falls.

The Paynims flee, abandoning the war;

Count Roland's left amid the field, unhorsed....

168

Now Roland feels that he is at death's door;

Out of his ears the brain is running forth.

Now for his peers he prays God call them all,

And for himself **St. Gabriel**'s aid implores;

Then in each hand he takes, **lest** shame befall,

His Olifant and Durendal his sword....

176

The County Roland lay down beneath a pine;

To land of Spain he's turned him as he lies,

And many things begins to call to mind:

Woe: Great sadness.

Peerage: Title or rank.

Wrath: Anger.

Jereeds: Wooden javelins or spears.

Scored: Scratched; slashed.

Veillantif: Roland's horse.

St. Gabriel: An archangel, one of the major biblical angels, who blows his trumpet to announce the Second Coming of Christ.

Lest: To avoid the risk that something happens.

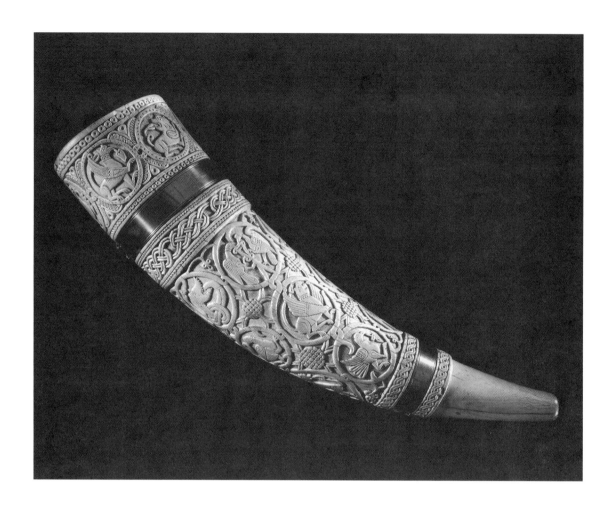

A Byzantine olifant like the one Roland had in *The Song of Roland*. © *The British Museum. Reproduced by permission.*

All the broad lands he conquered in his time,

And fairest France, and the men of his line,

And Charles his lord, who bred him from a child;

*He cannot help but **weep** for them and sigh....*

*His right-hand glove he's **tendered** unto Christ,*

And from his hand Gabriel accepts the sign.

Straightway his head upon his arm declines;

With folded hands he makes an end and dies.

*God sent to him His Angel **Cherubine**,*

*And great **St. Michael** of Peril-by-the-Tide;*

St. Gabriel too was with them at his side;

The County's soul they bear to Paradise.

Excerpt: "Ahi! Amours! Com dure departie/Alas, Love, What Hard Leave"

Alas, Love, what hard leave

I must take from the best lady

a man ever loved and served.

May God in his goodness lead me back to her

as surely as I part from her in grief.

Alas, what have I said? I do not part from her at all.

If my body goes to serve our Lord,

my heart remains all in her power.

For Him I go sighing into Syria,

for I must not fail my Creator.

Whoever fails him in this need for help—

do not doubt he shall fail in a greater need.

Let the great ones and the little ones know

*that there is the place for the great **chivalric** deed,*

where one wins Paradise and honor

and praise and the love of his beloved.

*God! we have long been brave in **idleness**,*

now we shall see who is brave in deed;

*we shall go to **avenge** the burning shame*

which ought to make us all angry and ashamed;

*for in our time the **Holy Place** is lost*

where God suffered death in agony for us;

if now we let our enemies remain,

our life will be forever more a life of shame.

Whoever does not want a life of misery here,

let him go die joyfully for God,

Weep: To cry.

Tendered: Offered, gave.

Cherubine: From "cherub," for angel.

St. Michael: Another archangel, or major angel, from the Bible.

Alas: Expression of sorrow.

Chivalric: Knightly and noble behavior; courage, honor, courtesy and a sense of justice.

Idleness: Doing nothing, having no direction. **Avenge:** To do harm in return for an injury.

Holy Place: Jerusalem and the Holy Land in Palestine.

for the taste of such a death is sweet and good,

*for which one wins the **precious** kingdom.*

No, not a single one of them will die into death,

but all will be born into glorious life.

Whoever comes back will be full of happiness;

honor to the end of his days will be his wife.

All clergy and aged men

who shall remain behind for charity

*will take part, all, in this **pilgrimage**,*

*and the ladies who will live in **chastity***

and keep faith with those who go.

*And if through evil **counsel** they do foolishness,*

they will do it with cowards, with scum,

for all good men will be gone on this voyage.

*God is **besieged** in his holy heritage;*

now we shall see how they come to his aid

whom he let loose from the dark prison

when he died on the Cross the Turks possess.

*Be sure of this: those who will not go bring **dishonor**
   on their name,*

unless they are poor, or old, or sick.

Those who are healthy, young, and rich

cannot stay home without shame.

*Alas! I go away **weeping** from my eyes,*

*I go where God wants to **amend** my heart,*

and I say I shall think of the best in this world

more than the voyage on which I part.

Precious: Having great value.

Pilgrimage: Religious journey.

Chastity: Virtue, purity.

Counsel: Advice.

Besieged: Surrounded.

Dishonor: Shame.

Weeping: Crying.

Amend: Change, make improvements on.

A manuscript illumination of troubadours, popular entertainers during the Crusades. © *Gianni Dagli Orti/Corbis. Reproduced by permission.*

What happened next...

The epic poems of the *chansons de geste* and the poems and songs of the troubadours led directly to the creation of longer works of fiction that became known as stories and novels. Such an advance can be seen in the *Decameron* (1348–53) of the Italian Giovanni Boccaccio and the Englishman Geoffrey Chaucer's *Canterbury Tales* (1387), both of which led to later poetry and true novels and both of which tell stories from the Crusades.

With the coming of the novel in the seventeenth and eighteenth centuries, a larger part of the public was able to read, and more views were shared. No longer could literature serve only propaganda. By the twentieth century great anti-war novels appeared, such as *All Quiet on the Western Front* by Erich Marie Remarque, Ernest Hemingway's *A Farewell to Arms,* Joseph Heller's *Catch-22,* and Kurt Vonnegut's *Slaughterhouse Five.* Literature was now able to service both sides of an argument.

Did you know...

- While troubadours and *trouvères* were generally aristocrats at first, in the later tradition they were people who wanted somehow to gain noble status, perhaps through a noble sponsor or through marriage. The *jongleurs,* or minstrels, on the other hand, continued to be mere entertainers, singing but also juggling and playing musical instruments. They often had to tour to earn an income and ultimately, in the late Middle Ages, joined together in guilds, or unions, to protect their status.

- Only about eleven troubadour songs are known from the First and Second Crusades. However, after 1160 the number of such songs and poems hugely increased, and hundreds of them were written down.

- So common was the theme of love in medieval songs that the name for German troubadours, *Minnesängers,* means "those who sing of love."

- Both the songs and epic poems of the Middle Ages that deal with the Crusades often compare the Muslims, or Saracens, to "dogs" or other animals and use the color

The First Troubadour

William IX of the French province of Aquitaine is considered by many to be the first troubadour, or performing poet and singer. A veteran of the First Crusade, he brought back with him songs he had heard in the Middle East. In fact, his artistic recordings were more successful than his deeds on the battlefield, for William was more a lover than a fighter. He pioneered songs about the loss of love as well as adventures with ladies, and he turned Aquitaine into a center for European culture, attracting other poets and singers. He also lived what he wrote: often married, when he grew tired of his wives, he would put them in a convent (religious institution for women) and take up with a new love.

His poetry and songs began a tradition of wandering poets and minstrels that lasted for almost two centuries, but he was better with words than he was managing rebellious nobles and governing his rich territories. William is perhaps best known to history, however, as the grandfather of Eleanor of Aquitaine, who became the ruler of the province, the queen of France, and the queen of England. She also kept the troubadour tradition alive in Aquitaine, and the idea of courtly love, or dignified and polite relations between men and women, grew out of her court, or royal household.

"black" to describe them. Muslims are also portrayed as sneaky in such poems, and not to be trusted, while the Christian knights are typically pure of heart and heroic.

Consider the following...

- How is Roland described in *The Song of Roland*? How is the Muslim leader Marsile described? How could such descriptions help promote bad feelings between the West and the Muslim world?

- Discuss how the author of "Ahi! Amours! Com dure departie" feels about those who do not join in the Crusade.

- If you were a writer of propaganda, what message would you use to persuade people to go to war? What medium (newspaper, television, film, word of mouth) and what sort of content ("news," movies, documentaries, novels, poetry, music) would you employ?

For More Information

Books

Golden, Frederick, ed. *Lyrics of the Troubadours and Trouvères.* New York: Doubleday, 1978.

Riley-Smith, Jonathan, ed. *The Oxford Illustrated History of the Crusades.* New York: Oxford University Press, 1995.

The Song of Roland. Translated by Dorothy L. Sayers. London: Penguin, 1957.

Web Sites

Cyrus, Cynthia J. "Introduction to Medieval Music." *The ORB: On-line Reference Book for Medieval Studies.* http://the-orb.net/encyclop/culture/music/orbmusic.html (accessed on August 4, 2004).

Moncrieff, Charles Scott, trans. "The Song Roland." *Online Medieval and Classical Library.* http://sunsite.berkeley.edu/OMACL/Roland/ (accessed on August 4, 2004).

The Muslim Call to Arms

Excerpt from "Poem on the Crusades" (twelfth century)

Originally written by Abu l-Musaffar al-Abiwardi; Reprinted in Ibn al-Athir's *The Perfect History*; Edited by C. J. Tornberg; Published in 1851–1876

Excerpt from Book of the Maghrib *(thirteenth century)*

Originally written by Ibn Said; Reprinted in *The History of the Mohammedan Dynasties in Spain*; Translated by Pascuual de Gayangoss; Published in 1840

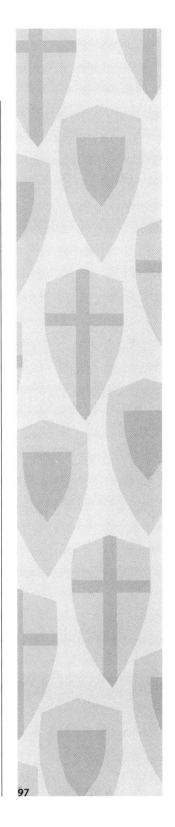

The Crusader invasion of 1096 to 1099 took the Muslims of the Middle East by surprise. Leaders of the Islamic world were busy with internal feuds and rivalries when the Christians arrived. The Seljuk Turks, who had established an empire in the Middle East, lost their strongest sultan, or leader, Malik-Shah, in 1092. With his death the Turks, who believed in sharing the rule in the family, scrambled to find leaders for all of the empire. But other Egyptian, Arab, and Syrian Muslims took advantage of this momentary chaos to try to extend their own territories at the expense of the Seljuks. Meanwhile, Muslims were also split into two religious branches: the Sunni Muslims, who followed the *Sunna,* or the words and acts of the prophet Muhammad, who had founded the religion, and the Shiites, who felt that religious authority could be passed on only by direct descendants or relatives of Muhammad. The Sunnis formed their base in Baghdad under what was known as the Abbasid caliphate, a religious and political dynasty ruling from Iraq. By the middle of the eleventh century, however, this dynasty had lost real power, and the Seljuk Turks actually ran things under the

Abbasid name. The other major branch of Islam, the Shiites, had their caliphate, or religious kingdom, in Egypt under the dynasty known as the Fatimids, from the name of Muhammad's daughter, Fatimah. There was also a breakaway Shiite sect (subgroup) the Nizari Ismaili, commonly known as the Assassins, who ruled in the mountains of Syria and Persia.

Thus the Muslim world was split politically and religiously when the Crusaders invaded. Fighting an enemy that was not organized, the Crusaders quickly captured the Holy Land, including Jerusalem, in 1099. The slaughter of Muslims and Jews in that city shocked the Muslim world when news got out. Slowly, as word spread, the Muslim people of the Middle East began to see the Christians as a common enemy. The Islamic faith has a principle known as *jihad,* which, on the personal level, is an effort to follow a religiously correct path in life and, on a more community-wide level, is a promise to protect the faith. This principle was soon adapted for a holy war against the infidel, a word used by both Christians and Muslims to indicate a nonbeliever in their particular faith.

The call to arms in the Islamic world was thus a matter of a religious message, as it was in Europe. Added to this, however, was the sense of anger at being invaded. Although the Holy Land of Palestine and Jerusalem, in particular, was sacred to Islam, Judaism, and Christianity, the fact was that Muslims had occupied it for centuries by the time of the First Crusade and looked on it as their homeland. As seen in the poem by an Iraqi poet of the eleventh and twelfth centuries, al-Abiwardi, there was shock and outrage at the sacking of Jerusalem in 1099 by the Crusaders. This poet was present in Baghdad when representatives from Syria and Palestine arrived to tell of the fall of Jerusalem and to ask for help from the Seljuk Turks to battle the invaders. For al-Abiwardi, the fall of Jerusalem was a sad occasion, but he also expressed anger at the fact that other Muslims did not react to this call to arms.

Ibn Said, a Muslim writer of the thirteenth century, describes the state of Islam in Spain in another excerpt in this section. However, his observations on the divisions and lack of unity between the Muslims that allowed for Christian domination in that peninsula could also be true for the Islamic world of the Middle East. It took strong leaders, including Nur al-Din and Saladin, to unite the Muslims in the twelfth century and respond to the Christian invasions. These calls to arms by Muslims were, in fact, similar to those of Pope Urban II when he urged the knights and nobles of Europe to stop fighting one another and come together to face a common enemy. For both the Christians and Muslims there was also the sense of a holy war, of fighting for God or Allah. And both used religious leaders to help spread the message of the holy war.

Things to Remember While Reading Excerpts about "The Muslim Call to Arms":

- When the Crusaders took Jerusalem in 1099, they spent two days killing all the inhabitants. Sources say that between forty thousand and seventy thousand people were killed, including women and children. After the slaughter, some Crusaders ripped open the bodies of the dead, hoping to find gold coins, which the Muslims supposedly swallowed to hide from their enemies. This massacre shocked the Muslims of the Middle East.

- The region of Syria and Palestine was not totally Muslim at the time of the First Crusade. There were large groups of native Christians living there, who practiced the Eastern Orthodox faith, the religion of the Byzantine Empire. There were also numerous Jews living in the region.

- When the Crusaders arrived, the Muslims at first mistook them for soldiers of the Byzantine Empire. Islam and that empire had long been enemies, so the Muslims were not too worried about such an invading force, for they thought they would not stay long.

- Islamic literary propaganda against the Crusaders often took the form of poetry, and it was written using the

The Byzantine church of Saint Simeon Monastery in Syria. The region of Syria and Palestine was not totally Muslim at the time of the First Crusade. © *John R. Jones/Corbis. Reproduced by permission.*

classical rules of Arab poetry established hundreds of years before the Crusades. Images of loss and destruction caused by the Crusaders thus often use the literary tradition of expressed sadness over the destruction of a campsite instead of a specific city or battle.

Excerpt: "Poem on the Crusades"

We have **mingled** blood with flowing tears, and there is no room left for pity.

To shed tears is a man's worst weapon when the swords stir up the embers of war.

Sons of Islam, behind you are battles in which heads rolled at your feet.

Dare you **slumber** in the blessed shade of safety, where life is soft as an orchard flower?

How can the eye sleep between the lids at a time of disasters that would waken any sleeper?

While your Syrian brothers can only sleep on the backs of their **chargers** or in vultures' bellies!

Must the foreigners feed on our **ignominy**, while you trail behind the train of a pleasant life, like men whose world is at peace?

When blood has been spilt, when sweet girls must for shame hide their lovely faces in their hands!

When the white swords' points are red with blood, and the iron of the brown **lances** is stained with gore!

At the sound of sword hammering on lance young children's hair turns white.

This is war, and the **infidel**'s sword is naked in his hand, ready to be **sheathed** in men's necks and skulls.

This is war, and he who lies in the tomb at Medina [Muhammad] seems to raise his voice and cry: "O sons of Hashim!

Mingled: Mixed.

Slumber: Sleep.

Chargers: Horses.

Ignominy: Disgrace, shame.

Lances: Long, wooden-shafted spears with steel points for use by mounted warriors.

Infidel: Unbeliever.

Sheathed: Put into a protective holster, or covering.

*I see my people slow to raise the lance against the enemy: I see the Faith resting on feeble **pillars**.*

For fear of death the Muslims are evading the fire of battle refusing to believe that death will surely strike them."

*Must the Arab champions then suffer with **resignation**, while the gallant Persians shut their eyes to their dishonour?*

Excerpt from Book of the Maghrib

*Andalus [the Iberian peninsula], which was conquered in the year 92 of the **Hijra**, continued for many years to be a dependency of the Eastern **Khalifate**, until it was snatched away from their hands by one of the surviving members of the family of Umeyyah [Umayyad], who, crossing over from Barbary, subdued the country, and formed therein an independent kingdom, ... During three centuries and a half, Andalus, governed by the princes of this dynasty,*

A fresco showing the Battle of Syria during the Crusades. © *Archivo Iconografico, S.A./Corbis. Reproduced by permission.*

Pillars: Refers to the pillars, or basic principles, of Islam.

Resignation: Acceptance of an undesirable result.

Hijra: The date when Muhammad left Mecca for Medina in 622 C.E.

Khalifate/Caliphate: General name for an Islamic state during the Crusades.

*reached the utmost degree of power and prosperity, until civil war breaking out among its inhabitants, the Muslims, weakened by internal **discord**, became everywhere the **prey** of the artful Christians, and the territory of Islam was considerably reduced, so much so that at the present moment the worshippers of the crucified [Christians] hold the greatest part of Andalus in their hands, and their country is divided into various powerful kingdoms, whose rulers assist each other whenever the Muslims attack their territories. This brings to my recollection the words of an eastern geographer who visited Andalus in the fourth century of the Hijra [tenth century A.D.], and during the prosperous times of the Cordovan Khalifate, I mean Ibnu Haukal Annassibi, who, describing Andalus, speaks in very unfavourable terms of its inhabitants.... "Andalus," he says, "is an extensive island, a little less than a month's march in length, and twenty and odd days in width. It ... is **amply** provided with every article which adds to the comforts of life; slaves are very fine, and may be **procured** for a small price on account of their abundance; owing, too, to the fertility of the land, which yields all sorts of grain, vegetables, and fruit, as well as to the number and goodness of its pastures in which innumerable flocks of cattle graze, food is exceedingly abundant and cheap, and the inhabitants are thereby plunged into **indolence and sloth**, letting mechanics and men of the lowest ranks of society overpower them and conduct their affairs. Owing to this it is really astonishing how the Island [i.e., peninsula] of Andalus still remains in the hands of the Muslims, being, as they are, people of vicious habits and low inclinations, narrow-minded, and entirely devoid of fortitude, courage, and the military accomplishments necessary to meet face to face the **formidable** nations of Christians who surround them on every side, and by whom they are continually **assailed**."*

Such are the words of Ibnu Haukal; but, if truth be told, I am at a loss to guess to whom they are applied. To my countrymen they certainly are not; or, if so, it is a horrible **calumny**, for if any people on the earth are famous for their courage, their noble qualities, and good habits, it is the Muslims of Andalus; and indeed their readiness to fight the common enemy, their constancy in upholding the holy **tenets** of their religion, and their endurance of the hardships and **privations** of war, have become almost proverbial.... As to the other **imputation**, namely, their being devoid of all senses, wisdom, and talent, either in the field or in administration, would to God that the author's judgment were correct, for then the ambition of the chiefs would not have been raised, and the Muslims would not have turned

Subdued: Gained control over.

Discord: Lack of agreement.

Prey: Helpless victim.

Amply: More than enough.

Procured: Gotten.

Indolence and Sloth: Laziness.

Formidable: Powerful.

Assailed: Attacked.

Calumny: False statement.

Tenets: Laws or basic principles.

Privations: Lack of basic essentials of survival, such as food and water.

Imputation: Accusation.

against each other's breasts and dipped in each other's blood those very weapons which God Almighty put into their hands for the destruction and annihilation of the infidel Christian. But, as it is, we ask—were those **Sultans** and **Khalifs** wanting in **prudence** and talents who governed this country for upwards of five hundred years, and who administered its affairs in the midst of foreign war and civil discord? Were those fearless warriors **deficient** in courage and military science who withstood on the frontiers of the Muslim empire the frightful shock of the innumerable infidel nations who dwell within and out of Andalus, ... all of whom ran to arms at a moment's notice to defend the religion of the crucified? And if it be true that at the moment I write the Muslims have been visited by the **wrath** of heaven, and that the **Almighty** has sent down defeat and shame to their arms, are we to wonder at it at a time when the Christians, proud of their success, have carried their arms as far as Syria and Mesopotamia, have invaded the districts **contiguous** to the country which is the meeting place of the Muslims, and the **cupola** of Islam, committed all sorts of **ravages and depredations**, and conquered the city of Haleb (Aleppo) and its environs ... ? No, it is by no means to be wondered at, especially when proper attention is paid to the manner in which the Andalusian Muslims have come to their present state of weakness and **degradation**. The ... Christians will rush down from their mountains, or across the plain, and make an **incursion** into the Muslim territory; there they will pounce upon a castle and seize it: they will ravage the neighbouring country, take the inhabitants captive, and then retire to their country with all the **plunder** they have collected, leaving, nevertheless, strong **garrisons** in the castles and towers captured by them. In the meanwhile the Muslim king in whose **dominions** the inroad has been made, ... will be waging war against his neighbours of the Muslims; and these, instead of defending the common cause, the cause of religion and truth,—instead of assisting their brother, will **confederate and ally** to deprive him of whatever dominions still remain in his hands. So, from a **trifling** evil at first, it will grow into an **irreparable calamity**, and the Christians will advance farther and farther until they **subdue** the whole of that country exposed to their inroads, where, once established and fortified, they will direct their attacks to another part of the Muslim territories, and carry on the same war of **havoc** and destruction.

Sultans: State rulers or leaders.

Khalifs/Caliphs: Islamic religious leaders.

Prudence: Caution.

Deficient: Lacking.

Wrath: Anger.

Almighty: In this context, the Muslim god, Allah.

Contiguous: Adjoining, next to.

Cupola: A rounded vault, forming a roof.

Ravages and Depredations: Acts of stealing, looting, and destruction.

Degradation: Being put in a low position.

Incursion: Invasion.

Plunder: Stolen goods.

Garrisons: Military outposts.

Dominions: Lands, territories.

Confederate and Ally: Join together.

Trifling: Small, insignificant.

Irreparable: Beyond repair.

Calamity: Disaster.

Subdue: Control, hold in check.

Havoc: Chaos and disorder.

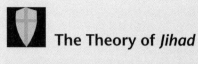

The Theory of *Jihad*

The idea of *jihad,* or holy war, was developed in works of Islamic law, such as the *Sharia,* and also is based on words from the Muslim holy book, the Qur'an (or Koran). It became one of the major duties of every believer in Islam. One Muslim writer noted, as quoted in Carole Hillenbrand's *The Crusades: Islamic Perspectives,* "the *jihad,* and rising up in arms in particular, is obligatory [required] for all able-bodied [believers], exempting no one, just as prayer, pilgrimage, and [payment of] alms are performed, and no person is permitted to perform the duty for another."

Literally, though, the word *jihad* means "struggle," and on the personal level it was meant to indicate the struggle each believer in Islam went through to lead a righteous or religious life. This struggle was a very personal one against the lower instincts in each of us. Over time, though, this understanding of the concept changed. As the external threat to the Islamic world grew, the principle of *jihad* was adapted as a call to arms of all the faithful to fight the infidel, be they the Byzantines in Asia Minor or the Crusaders who came from across the seas. Preachers at the mosques, or Islamic places of worship, became famous for preaching the holy war, with crowds of up to thirty thousand gathered inside and out to hear them.

What happened next...

The arrival of the Franks, as the Muslims called the Crusaders, led to the concept of *jihad* as a holy war against these invaders. Muslim writers criticized their fellow Muslims for softness and their leaders for being corrupt and allowing the Crusaders to establish strongholds in Palestine. Although the Seljuk Turks were not eager to come to the aid of Muslims attacked by the Crusaders, later dynasties were willing. The Zangids, a Turkish line that started with Zengi, preached a holy war against the Christian invaders. Under Zengi and his son, Nur al-Din, these Muslims took over Syria, and then, under one of their generals, Saladin, Egypt, too, was captured. Thus the Islamic world was unified for the first time, and during the twelfth century the power of the Crusader states formed in Palestine was steadily worn away. Jerusalem was taken back by Saladin in 1187, and, unlike the aftermath of the Christian victory in 1099, there was no slaughter of the inhabitants. Holy war had become a way of life in the Middle East by the end of the twelfth century.

Did you know…

- The Koran promotes the idea of *jihad,* but not always as it is thought of in the West. One quote from that holy book declares, "Prescribed for you is fighting, though it be hateful to you."

- The Muslims fought Crusaders with more than swords and bows and arrows. Zengi, the *atabeg,* or governor, of the city of Mosul and the Turkish Muslim leader who first organized Islam against the Crusaders, was more than a simple warrior. He established *madrassas,* or colleges, of Koranic studies as well as *khanqas,* or lodging houses, where traveling preachers and volunteers stayed as they spread the word against the Crusades.

- Other Muslim poets took up the need for a holy war after al-Abiwardi. Ibn al-Khayyat wrote verses for his patron, or sponsor, in Damascus that described the need for *jihad* against the Crusaders, and other anonymous poets similarly cry out in verse for revenge against the invading Franks. Also, the legal scholar and preacher al-Sulami wrote a report of the First Crusade in *Book of Holy War,* explaining the motives of the Crusaders and analyzing their goals clearly for other Muslims. Al-Sulami blamed defeat on the divided world of Islam and stated that the Crusaders planned to settle permanently in Jerusalem and the Holy Land.

Consider the following…

- Discuss some of the major divisions in the Muslim world that allowed the Crusaders to be so successful initially.

- What arguments and pleas does the author of "Poem on the Crusades" make to arouse his fellow Muslims to fight the Crusaders?

- The Christians and Muslims thought they were fighting for God or Allah, respectively, in the wars the West calls the Crusades. Explain how, if both parties had God on their side, there could have been a war at all. Who were the "good guys" and who the "bad guys"?

For More Information

Books

Hillenbrand, Carole. *The Crusades: Islamic Perspectives*. New York: Routledge, 2000

Ibn al-Athir. *Al-Kamil fi'l-tarikh*. Edited by C. J. Tornberg. Leiden, Holland, 1851–1876.

al-Makkari. *The History of the Mohammedan Dynasties of Spain*. Translated by Pascuual de Gayangoss. London: Oriental Translation Fund, 1840.

Web Sites

Abu l-Musaffar al-Abiwardi. "Poem on the Crusades." *Norton Anthology of English Literature*. http://www.wwnorton.com/nael/middleages/topic_3/alathir.htm (accessed on August 4, 2004).

Fordham University. "Book of the Maghrib, 13th Century." *Internet Medieval Sourcebook*. http://www.fordham.edu/halsall/source/maghrib.html (accessed on August 4, 2004).

Anti-Crusades

Excerpt from Annales Herbipolenses (1147)

**Originally written by an anonymous annalist in Würzburg;
Reprinted in *The Crusades: A Documentary History;* Translated by
James Brundage; Published in 1962**

Not everyone was convinced by the preaching for a holy war against the Muslims. There were those, as recorded by the following anonymous fifteenth-century historian of the German city of Würzburg, who saw other motives in this call to arms. Clearly, not every knight who "took the cross" and went off to fight the Muslim was a devout, or faithful Christian. Many went for individual profit, for new adventures, or just to escape boredom. Of course, the longer the Crusades lasted and the higher the cost in terms of lives and material, the more critics there were to the Crusader movement. And an unsuccessful mission, such as the Second Crusade (1147–49), as criticized in this excerpt, brought out even more negative opinion.

Things to Remember While Reading an Excerpt from *Annales Herbipolenses:*

- The rise in power of Zengi, the Turkish Muslim governor of Mosul, and his taking of the Crusader state of Edessa in 1144 led to the call for a Second Crusade.

- The medieval French clergyman Saint Bernard of Clair-vaux preached this Crusade in Europe. One of the most powerful and influential church figures of the twelfth century, Saint Bernard also had many enemies inside and outside the church.

- The Second Crusade was led by the king of France, Louis VII, and his wife, Eleanor of Aquitaine. The German emperor Conrad III also brought about twenty thousand troops, but he was defeated by the Muslims almost immediately.

Excerpt from Annales Herbipolenses

*God allowed the Western church, on account of its sins, to be **cast down**. There arose, indeed, certain **pseudo** prophets, sons of **Belial**, and witnesses of **anti-Christ**, who seduced the Christians with empty words. They **constrained** all sorts of men, by **vain** preaching, to set out against the **Saracens** in order to liberate Jerusalem. The preaching of these men was so enormously influential that the inhabitants of nearly every region, by common vows, offered themselves freely for common destruction. Not only the ordinary people, but kings, dukes, **marquises**, and other powerful men of this world as well, believed that they thus showed their allegiance to God. The **bishops, archbishops, abbots**, and other ministers and **prelates** of the church joined in this error, throwing themselves headlong into it to the great peril of bodies and souls.... The intentions of the various men were different. Some, indeed, **lusted** after **novelties** and went in order to learn about new lands. Others there were who were driven by poverty, who were in hard **straits** at home; these men went to fight, not only against the enemies of Christ's cross, but even against the friends of the Christian name, wherever opportunity appeared, in order to relieve their poverty. There were others who were oppressed by debts to other men or who sought to escape the service due to their lords, or who were even awaiting the punishment **merited** by their shameful deeds. Such men simulated a **zeal** for God and **hastened** chiefly in order to escape from such troubles and anxieties. A few could, with difficulty, be found who had not bowed their knees to **Baal**, who were directed by a holy and wholesome purpose, and who were **kindled** by love of the*

Cast Down: Fall on hard times.

Pseudo: Fake.

Belial: Satan, the devil.

Anti-Christ: In Christianity, a person who represents evil on Earth; a false Christ or an unbeliever in Christ.

Constrained: Persuaded.

Vain: Useless, meaningless.

Saracens: Muslims.

Marquises: Noblemen with a rank between duke and count.

Bishops, Archbishops, Abbots: Church officials of various ranks.

Prelate: A church official of high rank.

Lusted: Had a strong desire for.

Novelties: New or unusual things.

Straits: Conditions.

Merited: Deserved.

Zeal: Enthusiasm.

Hastened: Moved quickly.

Baal: A false god.

Kindled: Aroused, inspired.

divine majesty to fight earnestly and even to shed their blood for the holy of holies.

What happened next...

There was enough blame to go around after the failure of the Second Crusade. Saint Bernard of Clairvaux, however, was not apologizing for his role in promoting the Crusade. He blamed the Crusaders themselves for its failure. But the negative results of this Crusade had large consequences. The church, after all, had put all its resources into the mission and had their most powerful speaker, Saint Bernard, put his full energy and reputation into it. Kings also had supported this Crusade, unlike the First Crusade, in which only minor nobles led the battle. Still, it was a terrible failure, and the Muslims not only had scored major victories but also had gained self-confidence in their holy war against the Christian Crusaders.

Despite continued church support and propaganda for more Crusades, there was a widespread reaction against crusading as a large-scale movement, and there were no more major Crusades for forty years. With the defeat of the Second Crusade the appeal of the Crusader movement weakened. No longer did Crusaders go to stay in the Crusader states. Instead, they went almost as pilgrims, or religious travelers, fighting the "infidel," gaining a cleansing of their sins, and then returning to their homes in Europe. No amount of propagandizing could bring back the energy and blind faith witnessed in the first two Crusades.

Did you know...

• Recruitment, or getting an army in the field, was a major goal of propaganda for the Crusades.

One of the most powerful and influential church figures, Saint Bernard of Clairvaux preached on the Second Crusade. © *Michael Nicholson/Corbis. Reproduced by permission.*

Divine: God-like.

A sick pilgrim being treated during the Crusades. Although the church tried to discourage the elderly, women, children, and the sick from going on a Crusade, they were not always successful. *The Art Archive/ Bibliothéque Municipal Reims/ Dagli Orti. Reproduced by permission.*

- The church tried to discourage the elderly, women, children, and the sick from going on a Crusade. But they were not always successful in this effort. The People's Crusade of 1096, the Children's Crusade of 1212, and the Crusade of the Shepherds in 1251 were all examples of Crusader preaching that was too successful and inspired gangs of untrained people to fight the Muslims. Usually, these Crusades ended in tragedy for the participants.

- Knights, or noble soldiers, were the most important recruits for the Crusades. These mounted soldiers on horseback did most of the fighting, but there were many nonmilitary participants to bring along as well. Priests and other church officials were needed to pray for the soldiers before battle and at death; merchants were important to keep the armies supplied with food and arms; surgeons, youths to take care of the horses, and sailors to transport the armies were also necessary for a well-run Crusade.

- Kinship was an important tool of the recruiter. Sons often accompanied their fathers, brothers went with brothers, uncles and nephews took part together.

- The ties of lordship were also important in gathering an army. If a noble decided to go on Crusade, for example, then many of those in his circle or who were dependent on him also went. Thus it was important for the church to reach out to the higher nobility of kings, princes, and counts. By winning one, many might follow.

Consider the following...
- Explain how public opinion in Europe affected the progress of the Crusades.

- Discuss three reasons the writer of the excerpt from *Annales Herbipolenses* gave for men joining the Crusades. Which do you feel was the strongest motivation? Why?

- Discuss some of the negative results (from the Western point of view) of the failed Second Crusade. What do you think the Muslim victory in that same Crusade did for the spirit of the Islamic fighters?

For More Information

Books

Brundage, James, trans. *The Crusades: A Documentary History*. Milwaukee, WI: Marquette University Press, 1962.

Riley-Smith, Jonathan, ed. *The Oxford Illustrated History of the Crusades*. New York: Oxford University Press, 1995.

Web Sites

Fordham University "Annales Herbipolenses, s.a. 1147: A Hostile View of the Crusade." *Internet Medieval Sourcebook*. http://www.fordham.edu/halsall/source/1147critic.html (accessed on August 4, 2004).

"The Second Crusade." *The ORB: On-line Reference Book for Medieval Studies*. http://the-orb.net/textbooks/crusade/secondcru.html (accessed on August 4, 2004).

A Different View

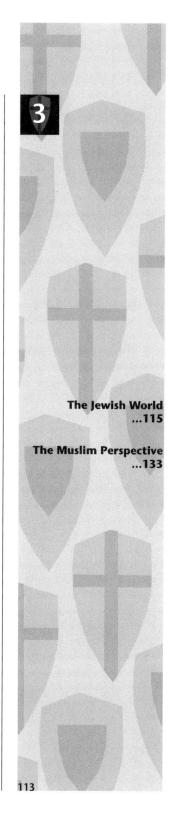

While much of the literature and historical documentation of the Crusades focus on the conflict between Christians and Muslims, there were other events, views, and perspectives of these times that are of equal importance. The followers of the Jewish religion, both in Europe and in the Middle East, were in many ways caught between the warring parties. Oppressed for centuries because of their supposed role in the death of Jesus Christ, Jews everywhere had a difficult time, but their situation in Europe was generally worse than it was in the Middle East. Often segregated, or separated, into ghettos away from Christians in European cities (and sometimes also from Muslims in the Middle East), the Jews of Europe generally were not allowed to own property, were restricted to certain specified occupations, and were forced to wear an identifying mark or badge to distinguish them from Christians. From being a largely agricultural people, they were compelled to live in cities in Europe where the professions of moneylending and commerce were the only ones open to them.

During the Crusades, the position of Jews in Europe was particularly dangerous, for traditional hatred bubbled over in the form of pogroms, or mass killings of Jews by Crusaders on their way to fight the infidel, that is, those people of the Middle East who did not believe in the Christian God. In the Middle East, things were often better for followers of the Jewish faith. Generally, in medieval times Jews were more integrated, or mixed, into normal life in the Middle East than in Europe. Although the Islamic holy book, the Qur'an (or Koran) calls the "children of Israel" unbelievers, it also states that Jews should be allowed to live in peace. The Jews in Europe and the Middle East did not take part in the great Crusader conflict between East and West, but they were often caught up in it, as were the Jews of Jerusalem, who were slaughtered along with all Muslims when the city fell to the Christian soldiers in 1099 during the First Crusade.

The histories of the Crusades have often presented the matter from the Christian point of view, neglecting that of the Muslims and also excluding other events in the Muslim world during the two centuries of religious warfare with the West. The Islamic world had a high culture at the time of the Crusades. Both in the arts and sciences, Muslim poets and scholars helped develop a civilization that was in many ways superior to that of the Christian kingdoms of the West at the same time. Muslims were especially strong in areas such as mathematics, medicine, and astronomy and thus looked at the European invaders, most of whom were uneducated, with a sometimes humorous and unflattering eye.

The Crusaders were not the only enemies the Muslims faced in the Middle Ages. Out of Central Asia the Mongols stormed into the Middle East in the twelfth and thirteenth centuries. These seminomadic warriors, led at first by the infamous Genghis Khan and later by his sons and other relatives, destroyed entire cities, killing all who fought against them. In many ways they presented a more dangerous threat than the Crusaders, and it was not until the middle of the thirteenth century that a Mamluk, or former slave warrior, from Egypt, Baybars, was able to stop their advance. All in all, the picture of Europe and the Middle East at the time of the Crusades was a very complex one, which cannot be seen solely in the restricted terms of a long-drawn-out conflict between Christians and Muslims.

The Jewish World

Excerpt from "The Crusaders in Mainz" (1096)

Originally written by Solomon bar Samson; Reprinted in *The Jew in the Medieval World: A Sourcebook, 315–1791*; Edited by Jacob Marcus; Published in 1938

Excerpt from "Las Siete Partidas: Laws on Jews" (1265)

Reprinted in *The Jew in the Medieval World: A Sourcebook, 315–1791*; Edited by Jacob Marcus; Published in 1938

Excerpt from The Itinerary of Benjamin Tudela: Travels in the Middle Ages *(late twelfth century)*

Originally written by Benjamin of Tudela; Translated by Marcus Nathan Adler; Published in 1907

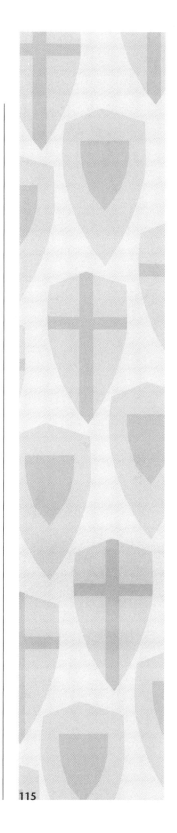

In the first excerpt of this section, the twelfth-century Jewish historian Solomon bar Samson describes how the enthusiasm for the Crusades bubbled over at the time of the First Crusade (1095–99), resulting in the killings of thousands of Jews in Germany as these Crusaders passed through the Rhineland on their way to the Holy Land. Considered infidels, the Jews became fair game for some Crusaders who wanted an excuse to loot the property of these people. Emich of Leiningen, a German noble, led one such group of soldiers who were responsible for the killings in the German city of Mainz that are described by Solomon bar Samson. Called Emico in this excerpt, this German Crusader was only one of several unscrupulous (without morals) leaders at the time of the First Crusade. A knight named Volkmar was another.

In the second excerpt, anti-Jewish laws are presented in "La Siete Partidas," or the Seven-Part Code, written in Castile, Spain, in 1265 but not put into effect until almost a hundred years later. In Spain during the thirteenth century the Jews were still too powerful and important to be mistreated. However, similar anti-Jewish, or anti-Semitic, laws were already in effect in much of the rest of Europe, many of them promoted by the Catholic Church. At the great meetings or councils of the church, called the Lateran Councils, laws were passed restricting the rights and privileges of Jews. The Fourth Lateran Council in 1215 made a law that Jews were forced to a wear a badge that separated them from Christians.

In the third excerpt, the twelfth-century Spanish (and Jewish) traveler Benjamin of Tudela provides an account of the situation of Jews not only in Europe but also throughout the Middle East at the time of the Crusades. On the whole, his travelogue shows that Jewish people were better off under Islamic rule than they were in Europe, where they were controlled by Christian laws. Benjamin provides a comparison, for example, of the harsh treatment of Jews in Constantinople, an Eastern Orthodox Christian city, with the kinder and more considerate treatment the Jewish people received at the hands of the caliph, or religious leader, of the Muslim city of Baghdad.

Things to Remember While Reading Excerpts from "The Jewish World":

- Crusaders were not always armies of noble, God-loving knights, as is shown in the excerpt about the killings of Jews in Mainz. Although the Jews sought safety in the palace of the archbishop, a high church official of the city, they were still killed by Emich/Emico and his men.

- There were numerous laws restricting the rights of Jews in Europe. Jews were forbidden to have Christian servants or to have relations of any sort other than business with Christians

- Innocent III, pope from 1198 to 1216, was the first pope who did not attempt to protect the Jews of Europe. In fact, Innocent III actually added to their persecution by passing a law that forced Jews to wear badges to separate them from the rest of society.

- Under Islamic law, the Jews did not have the full rights of Muslim citizens. They still had to pay taxes to the head of state. Depending on the ruler, however, Jews might or might not be segregated from the rest of society as they were in Europe.

- Despite or perhaps because of the persecution the Jews suffered, they developed a rich tradition of scholarship and philosophy. The Jewish diaspora, or spreading of Jewish people all over after they left the Holy Land, resulted in small and large communities of Jews throughout Europe and the Middle East, each with its own rabbi or scholarly and religious leader.

Excerpt from "The Crusaders in Mainz"

*It was on the third of **Siwan**... at noon, that Emico the wicked, the enemy of the Jews, came with his whole army against the city gate, and the citizens opened it up for him. Emico, a German noble, led a band of **plundering** German and French crusaders. Then the enemies of the Lord said to each other: "Look! They have opened up the gate for us. Now let us avenge the blood of 'the hanged one' [Jesus]." The children of the holy **covenant** who were there, **martyrs** who feared the Most High, although they saw the great multitude, an army numerous as the sand on the shore of the sea, still clung to their Creator. Then young and old **donned** their armor and **girded** on their weapons and at their head was **Rabbi** Kalonymus ben Meshullam, the chief of the community. Yet because of the many troubles and the **fasts** which they had observed they had no strength to stand up against the enemy.... Then came gangs and bands, sweeping through like a flood until Mayence [Mainz] was filled from end to end.*

*The **foe** Emico proclaimed in the hearing of the community that the enemy be driven from the city.... Panic was great in the town. Each Jew in the inner court of the bishop girded on his weapons, and all moved towards the palace gate to fight the crusaders and the citizens. They fought each other up to the very gate, but the sins of the Jews brought it about that the enemy overcame them and took the gate.*

*The hand of the Lord was heavy against His people. All the **Gentiles** were gathered together against the Jews in the courtyard to **blot out** their name, and the strength of our people weakened*

Siwan: The ninth month of the civil year; the third month of the religious year in the Jewish calendar (in May and June).

Plundering: Thieving and destroying.

Covenant: An agreement with God.

Martyrs: People who die for their faith.

Donned: Put on.

Girded: Secured with a belt.

Rabbi: Title of a Jewish religious leader and scholar.

Fasts: Periods of not eating.

Foe: Enemy.

Gentiles: Non-Jewish people.

Blot Out: Strike out, destroy.

Pope John Paul II places a signed note into a crack of the Wailing Wall in Jerusalem asking forgiveness for the persecution Catholics imparted on the Jews. © AP/Wide World Photos, Inc. Reproduced by permission.

Bishop: High Christian Church official.

Yoke: In this context, a burden or heavy weight.

Torah: Jewish holy book.

Nicked: Chipped.

when they saw the wicked Edomites overpowering them. [The Edomites were the traditional foes of the Jews; here, Christians are meant.] The **bishop**'s men, who had promised to help them, were the very first to flee, thus delivering the Jews into the hands of the enemy. They were indeed a poor support; even the bishop himself fled from his church for it was thought to kill him also because he had spoken good things of the Jews....

When the children of the covenant [the Jews] saw that the heavenly decree of death had been issued and that the enemy had conquered them and had entered the courtyard, then all of them—old men and young, virgins and children, servants and maids—cried out together to their Father in heaven and, weeping for themselves and for their lives, accepted as just the sentence of God. One to another they said: "Let us be strong and let us bear the **yoke** of the holy religion, for only in this world can the enemy kill us—and the easiest of the four deaths is by the sword. But we, our souls in paradise, shall continue to live eternally, in the great shining reflection [of the divine glory]."

With a whole heart and with a willing soul they then spoke: "After all it is not right to criticize the acts of God—blessed be He and blessed be His name—who has given to us His **Torah** and a command to put ourselves to death, to kill ourselves for the unity of His holy name. Happy are we if we do His will. Happy is anyone who is killed or slaughtered, who dies for the unity of His name.... He exchanges the world of darkness for the world of light, the world of trouble for the world of joy, and the world that passes away for the world that lasts for all eternity." Then all of them, to a man, cried out with a loud voice: "Now we must delay no longer for the enemy are already upon us.... Let him who has a knife examine it that it not be **nicked**, and let him come and slaughter us for the sanctification of the Only One, the Everlasting and then let him cut his own throat or plunge the knife into his own body." [A nick in the slaughterer's knife would make it ritually unfit.]

*As soon as the enemy came into the courtyard they found some of the very **pious** there with our brilliant master, Isaac ben Moses. He stretched out his neck, and his head they cut off first. The others, wrapped by their fringed praying shawls, sat by themselves in the courtyard, eager to do the will of their Creator. They did not care to flee into the chamber to save themselves for this **temporal** life, but out of love they received upon themselves the sentence of God. The enemy showered stones and arrows upon them, but they did not care to flee, and [Esther 9:5] "with the stroke of the sword, and with slaughter, and destruction" the foe killed all of those whom they found there....*

*The women there girded their loins with strength and **slew** their sons and their daughters and then themselves. Many men, too, **plucked up** courage and killed their wives, their sons, their infants. The tender and delicate mother slaughtered the babe she had played with.... The maidens and the young brides and grooms looked out of the Windows and in a loud voice cried: "Look and see, O our God, what we do for the **sanctification** of Thy great name in order not to exchange you for a hanged and crucified one...."*

*Thus were the precious children of **Zion**, the Jews of Mayence, tried with ten trials.... They stretched out their necks to the slaughter and they delivered their pure souls to their Father in heaven....*

The ears of him who hears these things will tingle, for whoever heard anything like this? Inquire now and look about, was there ever such an abundant sacrifice as this since the days of the primeval Adam? Were there ever eleven hundred offerings on one day, each one of them like the sacrifice of Isaac, the son of Abraham?

*Yet see what these martyrs did! Why did the heavens not grow dark and the stars not withdraw their brightness? Why did not the moon and the sun grow dark in their heavens when on one day, on the third of Siwan, on a Tuesday eleven hundred souls were killed and slaughtered, among them many infants and **sucklings** who had not **transgressed** nor sinned, and many poor, innocent souls?*

***Wilt Thou**, despite this, still restrain Thyself, O Lord? For thy sake it was that these numberless souls were killed. **Avenge** quickly the blood of Thy servants which was spilt in our days and in our sight. Amen.*

Excerpt from "Las Siete Partidas: *Laws on Jews*"

*LAW I. WHAT THE WORD JEW MEANS, AND **WHENCE** THIS TERM IS **DERIVED**.*

Pious: Very religious.

Temporal: Earthly.

Slew: Killed.

Plucked Up: Gathered.

Sanctification: Making holy.

Zion: The Jewish people.

Sucklings: Babies young enough to still be breast-feeding.

Transgressed: Broken a moral law.

Wilt Thou: Will You (meaning God).

Avenge: Do harm in return for harm done.

Whence: From where.

Derived: Originated.

A painting of a slaughter of the Jews in Mainz by the Crusaders. *Photograph by Vincente Cutanda y Toraya. Museo de Bellas Artes, Zaragoza, Spain/Bridgeman Art Library. Reproduced by permission.*

Dwell: Live.

Crucified: Put to death on the cross.

Contrary: Against.

Ordinances: Laws.

Exalting: Praising.

Disparaging: Criticizing.

A party who believes in, and adheres to the law of Moses is called a Jew.... The reason that the church, emperors, kings and princes permitted the Jews to **dwell** among them and with Christians is because they always lived, as it were, in captivity, as it was constantly in the minds of men that they were descended from those who **crucified** Our Lord Jesus Christ.

*LAW II. IN WHAT WAY JEWS SHOULD PASS THEIR LIVES AMONG CHRISTIANS; WHAT THINGS THEY SHOULD NOT MAKE USE OF OR PRACTICE, ACCORDING TO OUR RELIGION; AND WHAT PENALTY THOSE DESERVE WHO ACT **CONTRARY** TO ITS **ORDINANCES***

Jews should pass their lives among Christians quietly, ... practicing their own religious rites, and not speaking ill of the faith of Our Lord Jesus Christ.... A Jew should be very careful to avoid preaching to, or converting any Christian .... by **exalting** his own belief and **disparaging** ours. Whoever violates this law shall be put to death and lose all his property. And because we have heard it said that in some places Jews celebrated, and still celebrate, Good Friday, which commemorates the Passion of Our Lord Jesus Christ, by way of **contempt**: stealing children and fastening them to crosses, … we order that … if in any part of our **dominions** anything like this is done, and can be proved, all persons who were present when the act was committed shall be … arrested … and after the king **ascertains** that they are guilty, he shall cause them to be put to death in a disgraceful manner.…

LAW III. NO JEW CAN HOLD ANY OFFICE OR EMPLOYMENT BY WHICH HE MAY BE ABLE TO OPPRESS CHRISTIANS

Jews were formerly highly honored, and enjoyed privileges above all other races, for they alone were called the People of God. But for the reason that they disowned **Him**… and instead of showing Him reverence humiliated Him, by shamefully putting Him to death on the cross; it was proper and just that, on account of the great crime, … they should **forfeit** the honors and privileges which they enjoyed.… The emperors … considered it fitting and right that … they should lose all said honors and privileges, so that no Jew could ever afterwards hold an honorable position, or a public office by means of which he might, in any way, oppress a Christian.…

LAW IV. HOW JEWS CAN HAVE A SYNAGOGUE AMONG CHRISTIANS

A synagogue is a place where the Jews pray, and a new building of this kind cannot be **erected** in any part of our dominions, except by our order. Where, however, those which formerly existed there are torn down, they can be built in the same spot where they originally stood; but they cannot be made any larger or raised to any greater height, or be painted.… And for the reason that a synagogue is a place where the name of God is praised, we forbid any Christian to deface it, or remove anything from it, or take anything out of it by force; except where some **malefactor** takes refuge there.… Moreover, we forbid Christians to … place any **hindrance** in the way of the Jews while they are there performing their devotions according to their religion.…

*LAW V. NO **COMPULSION** SHALL BE BROUGHT TO BEAR UPON THE JEWS ON SATURDAY, AND WHAT JEWS CAN BE SUBJECT TO COMPULSION*

Saturday is the day on which Jews perform their devotions, and remain quiet in their lodgings and do not make contracts or trans-

Contempt: Disrespect.

Dominions: Territories.

Ascertains: Discovers.

Him: The capital letter used with "Him" refers to Jesus Christ, or the Lord.

Forfeit: Give up.

Erected: Built.

Malefactor: Criminal.

Hindrance: Obstacle.

Compulsion: Forced service.

act any business.... **Wherefore** we order that no judge shall employ force or any **constraint** upon Jews on Saturday, in order to bring them into court on account of their debts; or arrest them.... Jews are not bound to obey a summons served upon them on that day; and, moreover, we **decree** that any decision **rendered** against them on Saturday shall not be valid; but if a Jew should wound, kill, rob, steal, or commit any other offense like these for which he can be punished in person and property, then the judge can arrest him on Saturday....

LAW VI. JEWS WHO BECOME CHRISTIANS SHALL NOT BE SUBJECT TO COMPULSION; WHAT ADVANTAGE A JEW HAS WHO BECOMES A CHRISTIAN; AND WHAT PENALTY OTHER JEWS DESERVE WHO DO HIM HARM

No force or compulsion shall be employed in any way against a Jew to induce him to become a Christian; but Christians should convert him to the faith of Our Lord Jesus Christ by means of the texts of the **Holy Scriptures**, and by kind words.... We also decree that if any Jew or Jewess should voluntarily desire to become a Christian, the other Jews shall not interfere with this in any way, and if they stone, wound, or kill any such person, ... we order that all the murderers, or the **abettors** of said murder ... shall be burned.... We also order that, after any Jews become Christians, all persons in our dominions shall honor them; and that no one shall dare to **reproach** them or their descendants, by way of insult, with having been Jews....

LAW VII. WHAT PENALTY A CHRISTIAN DESERVES WHO BECOMES A JEW

Where a Christian is so unfortunate as to become a Jew, we order that he shall be put to death just as if he had become a **heretic**; and we decree that his property shall be disposed of in the same way that we stated should be done with that of heretics.

LAW VIII. NO CHRISTIAN, MAN OR WOMAN, SHALL LIVE WITH A JEW

We forbid any Jew to keep Christian men or women in his house, to be served by them; although he may have them to cultivate and take care of his lands, or protect him on the way when he is compelled to go to some dangerous place. Moreover, we forbid any Christian man or woman to invite a Jew or a Jewess, or to accept an invitation from them, to eat or drink together, or to drink any wine made by their hands.... We also order that no Jews shall

Wherefore: For that reason.

Constraint: Restriction.

Decree: Order.

Rendered: Made.

Holy Scriptures: The Bible.

Abettors: Helpers.

Reproach: Express disapproval.

Heretic: Believer in an unorthodox or unaccepted religious sect or group.

uarem herefef lu deoux

dare to bathe in company with Christians, and that no Christian shall take any medicine or **cathartic** made by a Jew....

LAW IX. WHAT PENALTY A JEW DESERVES WHO HAS **INTERCOURSE** WITH A CHRISTIAN WOMAN

Jews who live with Christian women are guilty of great **insolence** and boldness, for which reason we decree that all Jews who ... may be convicted of having done such a thing shall be put to death. For if Christians who commit **adultery** with married women deserve death on that account, much more do Jews who have sexual intercourse with Christian women, who are spiritually the wives of Our Lord Jesus Christ; ... nor do we consider it proper that a Christian woman who commits an offense of this kind shall escape without punishment. Wherefore we order that, whether she be a virgin, a married woman, a widow, or a common prostitute who gives herself to all men, she shall suffer the same penalty ... [i.e., confiscation of property, **scourging** , or death].

Manuscript illumination of heretics and Jews supposedly unable to hear the word of God. © *Gianni Dagli Orti/Corbis. Reproduced by permission.*

Cathartic: Digestive medicine.

Intercourse: Sexual relations.

Insolence: Being disrespectful.

Adultery: Sexual relations outside marriage.

Scourging: Being lashed with a whip.

LAW X. WHAT PENALTY JEWS DESERVE WHO HOLD CHRIS-TIANS AS SLAVES

A Jew shall not purchase, or keep as a slave, a Christian man or woman, and if anyone violates this law the Christian shall be restored to freedom ... although the Jew may not have been aware when he bought him, that he was a Christian; but if he knew that he was such when he purchased him, and makes use of him afterwards as a slave, he shall be put to death for doing so. Moreover, we forbid any Jew to convert a captive to his religion, even though said captive may be a **Moor**, *or belong to some other barbarous race. If anyone violates this law we order that the said slave who has become a Jew shall be set at liberty....*

LAW XI. JEWS SHALL **BEAR** *CERTAIN MARKS IN ORDER THAT THEY MAY BE KNOWN*

Many crimes and outrageous things occur between Christians and Jews because they live together in cities, and dress alike; and in order to avoid the offenses and evils which take place for this reason, ... we order that all Jews ... living in our dominions shall bear some distinguishing mark upon their heads, ... and any Jew who does not bear such a mark, shall pay for each time he is found without it ten **maravedis** *of gold; and if he has not the means to do this he shall receive ten* **lashes** *for his offense.*

Excerpts from The Itinerary of Benjamin Tudela: Travels in the Middle Ages

Constantinople

Constantinople is a busy city, and merchants come to it from every country by sea or land, and there is none like it in the world except Baghdad, the great city of Islam. In Constantinople is the church of Santa Sophia, and the seat of the **Pope** *of the Greeks, since the Greeks do not obey the pope of Rome. There are also churches according to the number of days of the year. A quantity of wealth beyond all telling is brought* **hither** *year by year as* **tribute** *from the two islands, and the castles and villages which are there. And the like of this wealth is not to be found in any other church in the world. And in this church there are pillars of gold and silver, and lamps of silver and gold more than a man can count. Close to the walls of the palace is also a place of amusement belonging to the king, which is called the Hippodrome, and every year on the anniver-*

Moor: North African and Spanish Muslim.

Bear: Wear.

Maravedis: Spanish coins.

Lashes: Strokes of the whip.

Pope: Leader of the Catholic Church, known as the "patriarch" in the Eastern Orthodox Church.

Hither: Here.

Tribute: Payment.

Benjamin of Tudela on his journey to the Middle East during the Crusades. *Mary Evans Picture Library. Reproduced by permission.*

sary of the birth of Jesus the king gives a great entertainment there. And in that place men from all the races of the world come before the king and queen with jugglery and without jugglery, and they introduce lions, leopards, bears, and wild **asses**, and they engage them in combat with one another; and the same thing is done with birds. No entertainment like this can be found in any other land.

This King Emanuel built a great palace for the seat of his government upon the seacoast.... He overlaid its columns with gold and silver, and **engraved** thereon representations of the battles before his day and of his own combats. He also set up a **throne** of gold and of

Asses: Donkeys.

Engraved: Decorated or carved on the surface.

Throne: Ceremonial chair for a king.

*precious stones, and a golden crown was suspended by a gold chain over the throne, so arranged that he might sit thereunder. It was **inlaid** with jewels of priceless value, and at night time no lights were required, for every one could see by the light which the stones gave forth…. From every part of the empire of Greece tribute is brought here every year, and they fill strongholds with **garments** of silk, purple, and gold…. It is said that the tribute of the city amounts every year to 20,000 gold pieces, **derived** both from the rents of shops and markets, and from the tribute of merchants who enter by sea or land.*

The Greek inhabitants are very rich in gold and precious stones, and they go clothed in garments of silk with gold embroidery, and they ride horses, and look like princes. Indeed, the land is very rich in all cloth stuffs, and in bread, meat, and wine.

Wealth like that of Constantinople is not to be found in the whole world. Here are also men learned in all the books of the Greeks, and they eat and drink, every man under his vine and his fig-tree….

*No Jews live in the city, for they have been placed behind an inlet of the sea. An arm of the sea of Marmora shuts them in on the one side, and they are unable to go out except by way of the sea, when they want to do business with the inhabitants…. And amongst them are **artificers** in silk and many rich merchants. No Jew there is allowed to ride on horseback. The one exception is the king's physician, and through whom the Jews enjoy considerable **alleviation** of their oppression. For their condition is very low, and there is much hatred against them, which is **fostered** by the **tanners**, who throw out their dirty water in the streets before the doors of the Jewish houses and defile the Jews' quarter. So the Greeks hate the Jews, good and bad alike, and subject them to great oppression, and beat them in the streets, and in every way treat them with **rigor**. Yet the Jews are rich and good, kindly and charitable, and bear their lot with cheerfulness….*

Tyre

*There is no harbor like [Tyre] in the whole world. Tyre is a beautiful city. It contains about 500 Jews, some of the scholars of the **Talmud**…. The Jews own sea-going vessels, and there are glassmakers amongst them who make that fine Tyranian glassware which is prized in all countries. In the vicinity is found sugar of a high class, for men plant it here, and people come from all over to buy it. A man can ascend the walls of New Tyre and see ancient Tyre, which the sea has now covered, lying at a stone's throw from*

Inlaid: Set into the surface.

Garments: Clothing.

Derived: Gotten.

Artificers: Manufacturers.

Alleviation: Easing, lessening.

Fostered: Promoted.

Tanners: Leather workers and dyers.

Rigor: Demanding, extreme conditions.

Talmud: A holy book for the Jews.

The Crusades: Primary Sources

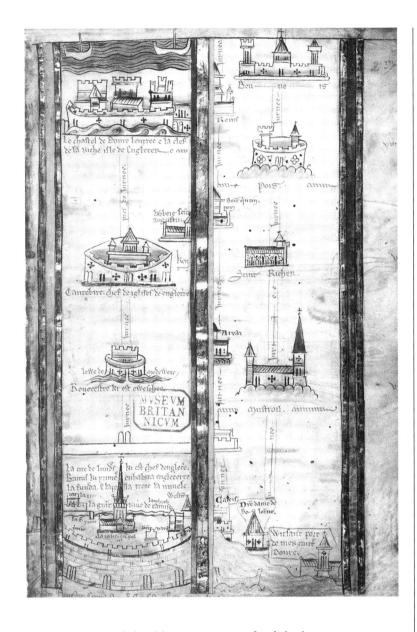

Medieval pilgrimage manuscript itinerary of the journey of Crusaders like the trip that Benjamin of Tudela describes in his manuscript. *The Art Archive/British Library/British Library. Reproduced by permission.*

*the new city. And should one care to go **forth** by boat, one can see the castles, market places, streets, and palaces, in the bed of the sea. New Tyre is a busy place of commerce, to which merchants flock from all quarters....*

Damascus

*Damascus, the great city, which is the **commencement** of the empire of Nur al-din, the king of the Togarmin, called Turks. It is a*

Forth: Out.

Commencement: Beginning.

*fair city of large extent, surrounded by walls, with many gardens and plantations, extending over fifteen miles on each side, and no district richer in fruit can be seen in all the world.… The city is situated at the foot of Mount Hermon. The Amana flows through the city, and by means of **aqueducts** the water is conveyed to the houses of great people, and into the streets and market places. The Pharpar flows through their gardens and **plantations**. It is a place carrying on trade with all countries. Here is a **mosque** of the Arabs called the Gami of Damascus; there is no building like it in the whole world, and they say that it was a palace of Ben Hadad. Here is a wall of crystal glass of magic workmanship, with **apertures** according to the days of the year, and as the sun's rays enter each of them in daily succession the hours of the day can be told by a graduated dial. In the palace are chambers built of gold and glass, and if the people walk around the wall is between them. And there are columns overlaid with gold and silver, and columns of marble of all colours … Three thousand Jews abide in this city, and amongst them are learned and rich men.*

Baghdad

*Baghdad, the great city and royal residence of the **Caliph Emir** al Muminin al Abbassi of the family of Mohammed. He is at the head of the Mohammedan religion, and all the kings of Islam obey him; he occupies a similar position to that held by the Pope over Christians.…*

*There the great king, Al Abbassi the Caliph (Hafiz) holds his **court**, and he is kind unto **Israel**, and many belonging to the people of Israel are his attendants; he knows all languages, and is well **versed** in the law of Israel. He reads and writes the holy language (Hebrew). He will not **partake** of anything unless he has earned it by the work of his own hands.… He is truthful and trusty, speaking peace to all men.*

*Within the **domains** of the palace of the Caliph there are great buildings of marble and columns of silver and gold, and carvings upon rare stones are fixed in the walls. In the Caliph's palace are great riches, and towers filled with gold, silken garments, and all precious stones.… [During the parade of **Ramadan**] He is accompanied by all the nobles of Islam dressed in fine garments and riding horses, the princes of Arabia, the princes of Togarma and Daylam (Gilan), and the princes of Persia, Media and Ghuzz, and the princes of the land of Tibet, which is three months' journey distant,*

Aqueducts: Elevated channels for water.

Plantations: Estates with crops.

Mosque: Muslim church.

Apertures: Openings.

Caliph: Religious/political leader in Islam.

Emir: Title of a Muslim and usually Arab ruler.

Court: The establishment of a ruler.

Israel: The Jewish people.

Versed: Knowledgeable.

Partake: Eat or drink.

Domains: Areas.

Ramadan: Ninth month of the Islamic year, when no food is eaten from sunset to sunrise.

and westward of which lies the land of Samarkand.... Along the road the walls are adorned with silk and purple, and the inhabitants receive him with all kinds of song and **exultation**, *and they dance before the great king who is styled Caliph....*

He built, on the other side of the river, on the banks of an arm of the Euphrates which borders the city, a hospital consisting of blocks of houses and **hospices** *for the sick poor who come to be healed. Here there are about sixty physicians' stores which provided from the Caliph's house with drugs and whatever else may be required. Every sick man who comes is maintained at the Caliph's expense and is medically treated. Here is a building called Dar-al-Maristan, where they keep charge of the* **demented** *people who have become insane in the towns through the great heat in the summer, and they chain each of them in iron chains until their reason becomes restored to them in the winter-time. Whilst they* **abide** *there, they are provided with food from the house of the Caliph, and when their reason is restored they are dismissed and each one them*

The minarets on a mosque. Benjamin of Tudela described mosques like the one pictured here in his manuscript of his journeys during the Crusades. © *Jose Fuste Raga/Corbis.*

Exultation: Celebration, triumph.

Hospices: Homes for the sick and dying.

Demented: Mentally ill.

Abide: Live, stay.

goes to his house and his home. Money is given to those that have stayed in the hospices on their return to their homes.... All this the Caliph does out of charity to those that come to the city of Baghdad, whether they be sick or insane. The Caliph is a righteous man, and all his actions are good.

*In Baghdad there are about 40,000 Jews, and they dwell in security, prosperity and honour under the great Caliph; and amongst them are the great **sages**, the heads of Academies engaged in the study of the law. In this city there are ten Academies.... In Baghdad there are 28 **synagogues**, situated either in the city itself or in Al-Karish on the other side of the Tigris, for the river divides the **metropolis** in two parts.*

Sages: Scholars.

Synagogues: Jewish churches.

Metropolis: City.

What happened next...

Jews continued to be persecuted in Europe during the time of the Crusades. With the Second Crusade in 1147, the Jewish people of Germany were once again set upon by Crusader forces before they left for the Holy Land. The famous church scholar Saint Bernard of Clairvaux, who preached the Second Crusade, had to go to Germany to try to stop this persecution. Again, just before the Third Crusade, the Jews of York, England, were attacked and killed by mobs of Christians.

The legal position of the Jews in Europe continued to worsen during and after the time of the Crusades. Jews were actually expelled from, or kicked out of, certain countries: this happened in France in 1182, in England in 1290, and in Spain in 1492. While the position of the Jew in the Middle East remained stable during much of the Middle Ages, it is obvious from the Arab-Israeli conflict of the twentieth and twenty-first centuries that the two peoples and two religions have difficulty sharing the limited living space of the region.

Did you know...

- Spain was the home for great Jewish scholars at the time of the Crusades. Maimonides was one of the most fa-

The Lateran Councils

The great conferences of the Catholic Church during the Middle Ages were held in the pope's palace on the Lateran Hill in Rome and so became known as the Lateran Councils. While the first two such councils dealt with internal policies of the church, the third, in 1179, and fourth, in 1215, deeply affected Jewish history in Europe.

With the Third Lateran Council, Jews were forbidden to have Christian servants, and Christians who lived with Jews even as renters were excommunicated, or expelled, from the church. This council also established that Christian testimony, or statements in legal matters, was considered above that of Jews, and punishment for usury, or unfair lending practices, was increased. There would be no Christian burial for those found guilty of usury. As a result, the role of moneylender, a necessary one in the Middle Ages, as it is in the modern world, became more and more reserved only for Jews.

The Fourth Lateran Council dealt with many bad practices within the Catholic Church, such as selling church offices. But it also passed a number of anti-Jewish laws. Nobles were forbidden to have Jewish officials working for them. Jews were also forced to pay extra taxes and to wear an identifying badge. Usually, the Fourth Lateran Council is thought of as a great moment in church history, when Pope Innocent III pushed through many reforms. But for the Jews, that council was a disaster.

mous Jewish scholars of the twelfth century, born in Cordova but forced to leave Spain when a radical Muslim group came to power.

• Benjamin of Tudela wrote of travels that took him not only to the Middle East but also, supposedly, as far as China and India. Scholars, however, believe that these sections of his travel guide were simply copied from reports of other travelers and that Mesopotamia, or modern-day Iraq, was his easternmost point of travel.

• Jewish occupations were tightly restricted in Europe. Because Jews could not own land, they were forced into commercial professions and into moneylending. As Christian doctrine, or law, looked at this occupation negatively, Jews were further criticized for taking up this job. In fact, Jews were caught in a no-win situation by such policies.

- The badges that Jews were forced to wear beginning in 1215 ultimately led to the armbands that Jews had to wear during World War II (1939–45), which made them targets in Nazi-controlled Europe.

Consider the following...

- Why do you think the Catholic Church passed anti-Jewish laws?

- In the course of his travels, Benjamin of Tudela was careful to record the size of Jewish communities throughout the Middle East. What does this tell you about the multicultural aspect of the region during the Middle Ages?

- During World War II (1939–45), it is estimated that more than six million Jews were killed by the Nazis. Explain how Europe's long tradition of anti-Semitism helped create an atmosphere that would make this possible.

For More Information

Books

Benjamin of Tudela. *The Itinerary of Benjamin of Tudela: Critical Text, Translation, and Commentary by Marcus Nathan Adler.* New York: Phillip Feldenheim, 1907.

Marcus, Jacob, ed. *The Jew in the Medieval World: A Sourcebook, 315–1791.* New York: JPS, 1938.

Web Sites

Fordham University. *Internet Jewish History Sourcebook.* http://www.fordham.edu/halsall/jewish/jewishsbook.html#The%20Jewish%20Middle%20Ages (accessed on August 4, 2004).

The Itinerary of Benjamin Tudela. http://chass.colostate-pueblo.edu/history/seminar/benjamin/benjamin1.htm (accessed on August 4, 2004).

"*Las Siete Partidas:* Laws on Jews, 1265." *Internet Medieval Sourcebook.* http://www.fordham.edu/halsall/source/jews-sietepart.html (accessed August 4, 2004).

"Soloman bar Samson: The Crusaders in Mainz, May 27, 1096." *Internet Medieval Sourcebook.* http://www.fordham.edu/halsall/source/1096jews.htm (accessed on August 4, 2004).

The Muslim Perspective

Excerpt from "On the Tatars" (1220–1221)

Originally written by Ibn al-Athir; Reprinted in *A Literary History of Persia*; Edited by Edward G. Browne; Published in 1902

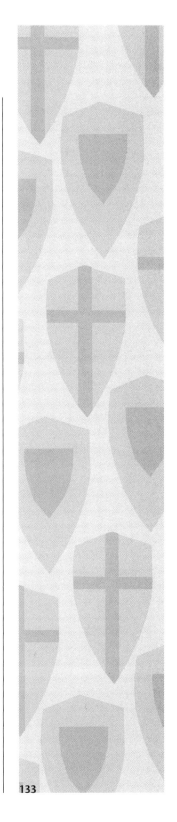

Numerous Arab chroniclers and historians told the story of the medieval Middle East from the Muslim point of view. From the twelfth and thirteenth centuries there were writers such as al-Sulami, Ibn al-Jawzi, Ibn Zafir, Abu Shama, Ibn Muyassar, and Ibn Wasil; from the fourteenth and fifteenth centuries al-Yunini, al-Nuwayri, al-Maqrizi, and Ibn Taghribirdi present the Muslim perspective on history. These authors provide historical accounts and memoirs, as well as official state biographies. Although their names mean little to Western readers, they form a cornerstone of Muslim and Arab writing from the Middle Ages. One of the best known of these historians is Ibn al-Athir. His book *The Perfect History,* sometimes also called *The Complete History,* is one of the most valuable medieval Muslim documents for modern researchers. From a literary family with two brothers who were also historians and writers, Ibn al-Athir has become one of the authorities on the Muslim world for historians, particularly for the time period from the Seljuk Turk invasion in the late eleventh century to the Mongol invasions of the thirteenth. As a historian, al-Athir had first-hand knowledge of events in the Middle East, serving with the Kurdish military leader Saladin in Syria. His histories thus blend personal experience with recorded annals (chronologies).

Ibn al-Athir is an example of someone who practiced anecdotal history, or history told through personal story. Arab writers included a wide range of styles and approaches. One highly entertaining early chronicler was Usamah ibn Munqidh, whose *An Arab-Syrian Gentleman and Warrior in the Period of the Crusades* provides the modern reader with an interesting and sometimes humorous look at the Crusaders of the twelfth century from the Muslim point of view. From that perspective, these Christian soldiers were not always the fair-fighting knights they said they were. The Franks, as the Muslims called the Crusaders, might be fierce warriors, as Usamah shows, but they were not very cultured or well-educated people. Usamah, like many other Arab writers, found the Crusaders uncivilized and uneducated. He delighted in stories of Crusader or Frankish doctors using axes to cut off injured limbs, killing the patient in the process. He also made fun of the court system of the Franks, who were fond of dunking suspects into barrels of water to gain a confession. Such a legal system presented a no-win situation for the poor suspect: those who did not confess ended up dying in the process, but were found innocent. And those who confessed to their crime, whether because they were guilty or to avoid drowning, were then condemned to death. Usamah's is only one such voice among dozens, like that of Ibn al-Athir excerpted below, that provides a fascinating insight into the minds of Muslims of the Middle Ages and into the events that shaped the age.

In this section's excerpt, Ibn al-Athir tells of a threat to the Muslims of the Middle East other than the Crusaders—namely, the Mongols. Born in 1160, Ibn al-Athir wrote a history of the world up to 1232, the year before his death. In *The Perfect History,* al-Athir calls the Mongols the Tatars, but they have also been referred to as Tartars. These Mongols came out of Central Asia and were initially led by Genghis Khan. They captured large sections of Asia Minor, Iraq, and Syria and were an enormous threat to Islam in the thirteenth century. Al-Athir gives a feeling for their fierce way of waging war in this excerpt.

Things to Remember While Reading the Excerpt from "The Muslim Perspective":

- The fierce invading Mongols were also known as Tatars or Tartars. Some believe that the name comes from *Ta-Tan*, a term of disrespect the Chinese may have given to the Mongols who conquered them. In the modern world the term is used for all the Turkish-speaking people of Europe and Asia.

- The Mongols originally lived in the Gobi Desert of China, north of the Himalayas.

- The Mongols were greatly feared because they showed no mercy to those who resisted them. Although the historian Ibn al-Athir writes about Mongol advances in Persia, the worse was yet to come for Islam. Under Hulagu Khan the Mongols took Baghdad in 1258. Some historians say that they massacred as many as eight hundred thousand of the city's inhabitants, including the caliph, or religious leader, and also destroyed large sections of the city. The sack of Baghdad almost put an end to Arab civilization.

Excerpt from "On the Tatars"

*For some years I continued averse from mentioning this event, **deeming** it so horrible that I shrank from recording it and ever withdrawing one foot as I advanced the other. To whom, indeed, can it be easy to write the announcement of the death-blow of Islam and the Muslims, or who is he on whom the remembrance thereof can weigh lightly? O would that my mother had not born me or that I had died and become a forgotten thing ere this **befell**! Yet, **withal** a number of my friends urged me to set it down in writing, and I hesitated long, but at last came to the conclusion that to omit this matter could serve no useful purpose.*

*I say, therefore, that this thing involves the description of the greatest catastrophe and the most **dire calamity** (of the like of which days and nights are innocent) which befell all men generally, and the Muslims in particular; so that, should one say that the world, since God Almighty created Adam until now, has not been **afflicted** with the like thereof, he would but speak the truth. For indeed history does not contain anything which approaches or comes near unto it. For of the most grievous calamities recorded was what **Nebuchadnezzar** inflicted on the children of Israel by his slaughter of them and his destruction of Jerusalem; and what was Jerusalem in comparison to the countries which these **accursed miscreants** destroyed, each city of which was double the size of Jerusalem? Or*

Deeming: Regarding.

Befell: Happened to.

Withal: Nevertheless.

Dire: Very serious.

Calamity: Tragedy.

Afflicted: Caused pain.

Nebuchadnezzar: Ancient king of Babylonia.

Accursed: Being under a curse.

Miscreants: People who behave viciously.

what were the children of Israel compared to those whom these *slew*? For **verily** those whom they massacred in a single city exceeded all the children of Israel. **Nay**, it is unlikely that mankind will see the like of this calamity, until the world comes to an end and perishes, except the final outbreak of **Gog and Magog**.

For even **Antichrist** will spare such as follow him, though he destroy those who oppose him, but these **Tatars** spared none, slaying women and men and children, ripping open pregnant women and killing unborn babes. Verily to God do we belong, and unto Him do we return, and there is no strength and no power save in God, the High, the Almighty, in face of this catastrophe, whereof the sparks flew far and wide, and the hurt was universal; and which passed over the lands like clouds driven by the wind. For these were a people who emerged from the confines of China, and attacked the cities of Turkestan, like Kashghar and Balasaghun, and **thence** advanced on the cities of Transoxiana, such as Samarqand, Bukhara and the like, taking possession of them, and treating their inhabitants in such **wise** as we shall mention; and of them one division then passed on into Khurasan, until they had made an end of taking possession, and destroying, and slaying, and plundering, and thence passing on to Ray, Hamadan and the Highlands, and the cities contained therein, even to the limits of Iraq, whence they marched on the towns of Adharbayjan and Arraniyya, destroying them and slaying most of their inhabitants, of whom none escaped save a small **remnant**; and all this in less than a year; this is a thing whereof the like has not been heard.…

These Tatars conquered most of the **habitable** globe, and the best, the most **flourishing** and most populous part thereof, and that whereof the inhabitants were the most advanced in character and conduct, in about a year; nor did any country escape their devastations which did not fearfully expect them and dread their arrival.

Moreover they need no **commissariat**, nor the **conveyance** of supplies, for they have with them sheep, cows, horses, and the like **quadrupeds**, the flesh of which they eat, **naught** else. As for their beasts which they ride, these dig into the earth with their hoofs and eat the roots of plants, knowing naught of barley. And so, when they **alight** anywhere, they have need of nothing from without. As for their religion, they worship the sun when it rises, and regard nothing as unlawful, for they eat all beasts, even dogs, pigs, and the like; nor do they recognise the marriage-tie, for several men are in marital relations with one woman, and if a child is born, it knows not who is its father.

Slew: Killed.

Verily: Certainly.

Nay: No.

Gog and Magog: Two nations in the Bible that are led by Satan and that fight the Kingdom of God in a final battle.

Antichrist: The devil, Satan.

Tatars: Tartars, or Mongols.

Thence: From there, as a result.

Wise: Way or manner.

Remnant: Those left over or remaining.

Habitable: Able to be lived in.

Flourishing: Wealthy and productive.

Commissariat: A military department to supply food.

Conveyance: Transport.

Quadrupeds: Four-legged animals.

Naught: Nothing.

Alight: Arrive.

Wrought: Committed.

Therefore Islam and the Muslims have been afflicted during this period with calamities wherewith no people hath been visited. These Tatars (may God confound them!) came from the East, and **wrought** *deeds which horrify all who hear of them, and which you shall, please God, see set forth in full detail in their proper connection. And of these was the invasion of Syria by the Franks (may God curse them!) out of the West, and their attack on Egypt, and occupation of the port of Damietta therein, so that Egypt and Syria were* *like to be conquered by them, but for the grace of God and the help which He **vouchsafed** us against them, as we have mentioned under the year 614 [A.D. 1217–18]. Of these, moreover, was that the sword was drawn between those who escaped from these two foes, and **strife** was rampant, as we have also mentioned: and verily unto God do we belong and unto Him do we return! We ask God to vouchsafe victory to Islam and the Muslims, for there is none other to aid, help, or defend the True Faith....*

*Stories have been related to me, which the hearer can scarcely credit, as to the terror of the Tatars, which God Almighty cast into men's hearts; so that it is said that a single one of them would enter a village or a quarter wherein were many people, and would continue to slay them one after another, none daring to stretch forth his hand against this horseman. And I have heard that one of them took a man captive, but had not with him any weapon wherewith to kill him; and he said to his prisoner, "Lay your head on the ground and do not move," and he did so, and the Tatar went and fetched his sword and slew him therewith. Another man related to me as follows: "I was going," said he, "with seventeen others along a road, and there met us a Tatar horseman, and **bade** us bind one another's arms. My companions began to do as he bade them, but I said to them, 'He is but one man; wherefore, then, should we not kill him and flee?' They replied, 'We are afraid.' I said, 'This man intends to kill you immediately; let us therefore rather kill him, that perhaps God may deliver us.' But I swear by God that not one of them dared to do this, so I took a knife and slew him, and we fled and escaped." And such occurrences were many.*

Vouchsafed: Gave, provided.

Strife: Conflict.

Bade: Ordered.

What happened next...

The dual threats to Islam, Crusaders and Mongols, were eliminated by the Mamluks of Egypt, a slave dynasty. The sultan, or ruler, of Egypt had a long tradition of using such slave warriors. But in the middle of the thirteenth century these elite soldiers actually took over Egypt, led by their new sultan, Baybars. This amazing soldier and statesman fought and defeated the Mongols at the Battle of Ayn Jalut in Palestine in 1260 and then turned his attention to the Crusaders. By the time of Baybars's death in 1277, he had restricted the Crusaders to a few remaining strongholds. His successors, the sultans next in line, finished off the job he had started, defeating the Crusaders at Acre in 1291 and pushing them out of the Middle East totally. There is a certain irony that Islam, one of the most cultured civilizations of its day, was saved by these former slaves, mostly uneducated and only recent converts to the religion.

Did you know...

• Though the Crusaders liked to think of themselves as more civilized than their Muslim enemies, this was not actually the case. In general, the educational level of residents of the medieval Middle East was higher than that of people in Europe. The founder of Islam, Muhammad, said that "the ink of scholars is more precious than the blood of martyrs." He ordered that public education be made available to believers in Islam. Also, the rise of mass-produced paper helped create private and public libraries, and the use of so-called Arabic numerals (originally from India) made mathematics easier than with the Roman numerals.

• Islam preserved the knowledge of the past. Medieval Muslim scholars such as Avicenna, Avempace, and Averroës translated and commented on the works of the great Greek philosophers, thus saving that intellectual tradition for the world.

• Works such as Ibn al-Athir's history are very hard to translate into English from their original Arabic language and not only because of the different alphabet. In Arabic there is no system of capitalization, and therefore it is often difficult to tell the difference between a common noun and someone's proper name. Another difficulty for the translator is that twenty-two of twenty-eight of the characters of the Arabic alphabet are recognized by the presence or absence of dots above or below the characters. More possible confusion is caused by the fact that there are no ending quotation marks in Arabic to show when a direct quote stops.

- The Muslims usually referred to the Crusaders as Franks. Sometimes in other sources this is written "Franj." This name was used because at the time of the First Crusade (1095–99), most of these Christian soldiers came from French- speaking lands. Although, later, Englishmen, German, and Italians made up larger groups among the Crusaders, the Muslims continued to call them all Franks.

- Taking advantage of disunity among their enemies, the Mongols created an empire that stretched from Korea and the Pacific all the way over to Georgia, Armenia, and Hungry in the west. Only two hundred thousand people strong, the Mongols were able to defeat much larger countries, such as China, with a population at the time of one hundred million. Theirs was the largest empire in world history, ruling an area of almost fourteen million square miles.

- In addition to the Mongols, the other large group of the thirteenth century in the Middle East was the Mamluk empire. Mamluk comes from the Arabic word "to own," and reminds us of the Mamluk's slave history.

- After defeating both Mongols and Crusaders, the Mamluks created an empire in the Middle East consisting of Egypt, Palestine, Syria, and parts of present-day Iraq and Asia Minor. Their slave dynasty outlasted many of the more "legitimate" dynasties of the region, remaining in direct power from about 1250 to 1517, when the Ottoman Turks defeated them. However, the Mamluks

Enemies Everywhere

The Islamic world faced numerous enemies in the thirteenth century. As we have seen, the Crusaders presented one threat, for they maintained their Crusader states along the eastern Mediterranean and also had occasional reinforcements from Europe. Small battles and full-blown Crusade wars continued to disrupt the Middle East throughout the thirteenth century. The Mongols provided another real threat, as Ibn al-Athir explained. However, there was also a third danger from the north during the early decades of the thirteenth century.

With the breakup of the Seljuk Turk empire, another Turkish tribe, the Khwarismian Turks, gained their independence and began pushing southward. A leader of these Turks, Muhammad Shah, though a convert to Islam, was no friend to the old and settled Muslim rulers. In 1217 he pushed his mounted army to Baghdad and chased out the caliph, or religious and political leader, Nasir. These Turks were great warriors and were then at the height of their power, but they made a mistake when they expanded eastward toward Russia and killed a couple of representatives from the Mongols and Genghis Khan. In 1221 Genghis Khan conquered these Khwarismian Turks and forced them afterward to fight in his huge Mongol army, the Golden Horde.

continued to rule in Egypt under the Turks until the arrival of the French and Napoleon Bonaparte in 1798.

Consider the following...

- Islam was threatened by two enemies in the thirteenth century. Discuss who these enemies were and which you think was the greater threat and why.

- What do you think might have happened if the Mongols had not been stopped in the Middle East? How might the world be different now?

- Discuss how an educated Muslim at the time of the Crusades might describe the invading Crusaders. How did the Crusaders see the Muslims?

For More Information

Books

Browne, Edward G., ed. *A Literary History of Persia.* Cambridge: Cambridge University Press, 1902.

Usamah ibn-Munqidh, *An Arab-Syrian Gentleman and Warrior in the Period of the Crusades: Memoirs of Usamah ibn-Munqidh.* Translated by Philip K. Hitti. New York: Columbia University Press, 2000.

Web sites

"Ibn al-Athir: On the Tatars, 1220–1221 CE." *Internet Medieval Sourcebook.* http://www.fordham.edu/halsall/source/1220al-Athir-mongols.html (accessed on August 4, 2004).

A Matter of Faith

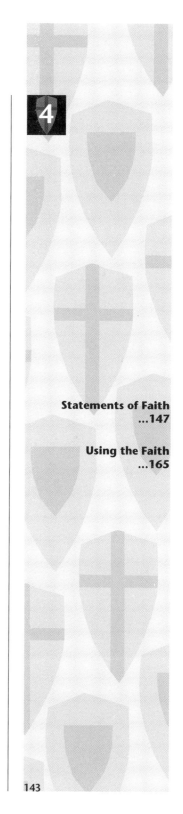

4

Historians have given many interpretations and causes for the two centuries of war between Christianity and the Islamic world that we know as the Crusades. There were, of course, political concerns, with the Catholic pope wanting to gain power in the Eastern Empire, also known as the Byzantine Empire, the rival Christian empire of the time. Princes, kings, and emperors also had a desire to increase the size of their holdings and perhaps even create new empires in the Middle East. Economic reasons were also important, as many people and cities made a good living off the Crusades, transporting the soldiers and setting up new areas for trade. But most important, the Crusades were about religion and about which religion should control the holy sites in the city of Jerusalem, sacred to Islam and Christianity (as well as Judaism). It was this competition between religions, the debate over whose god was best, that continued to drive the Crusaders and Muslim fighters alike.

The most recent of the great religions, Islam came into existence in the late sixth and early seventh centuries. Christianity thus had about six hundred years head start, and

Judaism, the third great religion of the Middle East and Europe, was older than both, stemming from perhaps two thousand years before the birth of Jesus Christ. But Islam spread quickly. Its founder, Muhammad, believed that he was visited by the angel Gabriel when he was about forty years old and that the angel told him to become a messenger of the word of Allah, or God. All those who followed or submitted to the word of Allah were known as Muslims; the name of the religion, Islam, means "to submit." In certain ways Islam is similar to Christianity, especially in that the faithful are always looking for new members or converts from other religions.

Christianity's holy book is known as the Bible; Muslims have the Qur'an, or Koran, a book that pays special attention to leading a moral and proper life. Islamic law covers practical matters, from what one should eat to how one should deal with the poor and with other Muslims. Written in Arabic, the Koran played a large part in making that language a gathering point for the Islamic world, for the Koran was not intended to be translated. Instead, the faithful were meant to read it in its original language and also to pray in Arabic. As Islam spread in its first four centuries, the central position of the Koran and of Arabic made the religion not only a spiritual movement but also a cultural, or Arab, one. By the time of the Crusades the Islamic world had already reached and just passed the high point of its civilization and empire, controlling lands from India to Asia Minor, from Iraq to Arabia, and from Egypt and North Africa to Spain and southern Italy.

Christianity was also on the rise at the time of the Crusades. In Europe, there was a competition between the leader of the church, the pope, and the kings and emperors who were establishing their kingdoms. The pope and the kings of France and England, as well as the German emperor, were rivals for power in medieval Europe. The church controlled much of the cultural life of the time and also sought to establish itself as the messenger of God on Earth. As far as the popes were concerned, all power, spiritual and temporal (political), came from them.

The teachings of the Bible and the first books of the New Testament, or the Gospels, had a strong influence on both nobles and common people during the Middle Ages.

The miracles of the church were widely accepted and kept the faithful together and believing. However, even in the Middle Ages there were those who searched for their own private forms of religion. Such skeptics and part-believers were found, as we shall see, in both the Christian and Muslim worlds.

The power of religion was used to bring the faithful of both Christianity and Islam to battle. Both sides saw their warriors as soldiers of God, and both spoke of fighting battles for their religion. In the West this was known as a holy war, or Crusade, while in the Muslim world it was called *jihad,* also meaning holy war. The Crusades were an expensive adventure, and to finance it the church often taxed the faithful. Early states of Europe were not organized to allow such taxation of the common people, but the church, with its local priests, was. Also, faith could be used to create elite groups of fighters. From the time of the First Crusade (1095–99), Crusaders were promised to have their sins forgiven in return for their service. This use of faith in wartime was extended even further with the creation of religious military orders, such as the Knights Templars and Knights Hospitallers in the early twelfth century. Faith and religion have continued to play prominent parts in conflicts throughout human history. Most of the time, all participants in a war think that they have God on their side.

Statements of Faith

Excerpt from The Koran *(c. seventh century)*
Translated by N. J. Dawood; Published in 1990

Excerpt from "The Holy Light; How It Descends upon the Holy Sepulchre," in The Pilgrimage of the Russian Abbot Daniel in the Holy Land *(1106–1107)*
Originally written by Abbot Daniel; Published in 1888

Excerpt from "The Prior Who Became a Moslem," in Book of a Thousand Nights and a Night *(c. 1000—1400)*
Reprinted in *The Arabian Nights*; Translated by Sir Richard Francis Burton; Published in 1997

"Profession of Faith" (1120)
Originally written by Omar Khayyam; Reprinted in *The Sacred Books and Early Literature of the East*; Edited by Charles F. Horne; Published in 1917

The four excerpts of this section examine different statements about the power of faith and belief. The first is from the Koran, or Islamic holy book, also known as the Qur'an. The teachings and prayers in the Koran were supposedly spoken to Muhammad by God, and it is the source of the major principles of Islam. The Koran was intended to be recited, or spoken aloud, and was written down only in the seventh century, several decades after the death of Muhammad. The excerpt included here celebrates an early victory of the followers of Muhammad, perhaps the taking of Mecca in 630. Muhammad was born there in about 570 and worked as a trader until he had a vision that he was meant to be the messenger of God in a new religion. Muhammad was forced to leave Mecca in 622 for the city of Medina. The Muslim calendar begins from this date, the time of the *hijra* or "flight." Muhammad quickly gained support in Medina, and by 630 Mecca surrendered to him.

The second excerpt describes a miraculous event that takes place every Easter at the tomb, or burial place, of Jesus Christ in Jerusalem. This event is known as the Holy Light, or

An illustration from *Arabian Nights*. *Private Collection/ Roger Perrin/Bridgeman Art Library. Reproduced by permission.*

Holy Fire, that supposedly illuminates, or lights up, Christ's tomb. Pilgrims, or religious visitors, come in huge numbers to witness this event. This was true even at the time when the Russian holy man Abbot Daniel paid his visit to Jerusalem in 1106 and 1107. In fact, this miracle of a dancing light that appears the Saturday before Easter was first recorded in the fourth century. During the ceremony the candles that the faithful carry to the church are lit spontaneously by this mysterious light, with no one putting a match to them. Such miracles were more usual in the medieval church and were a powerful influence on the faithful.

The power of miracles in prompting a change of religion is seen in the third excerpt, "The Prior Who Became a Moslem" a tale from the *Book of a Thousand Nights and a Night*. This anonymous gathering of stories from all over the Middle East and even India is also known as *The Thousand and One Nights* or *The Arabian Nights*. It has not been determined exactly when or where these tales began, but it is thought they were collected starting in about the middle of the tenth century. New tales continued to be added after that date, and events and names from many centuries and many states of the Middle East can be found in them. Perhaps the best-known tales in the West are ones such as "Ali Baba," "Sinbad," and "Aladdin," but these are only the tip of a very deep and rich iceberg of literature. Some collections have all one thousand and one tales, others fewer. The first European editions of this collection did not appear until 1704.

In the last excerpt of this section, another sort of faith is on display. Omar Khayyam, an eleventh- and twelfth-century Persian mathematician and poet, is best known for his collection of verses called the *Rubaiyat*. In his poem, "Profession of Faith," he maps out his own version of what he believed in, somewhere between Islam and Christianity. For

Khayyam, enjoying this world of earthly pleasures seems more important than a promised heaven after death. Such a philosophy was not, however, very common in the Middle Ages, a time when religion drove the major events.

Things to remember while reading excerpts from "Statements of Faith":

- Unlike the Bible, the Koran refers to religious and historical events but seldom provides narrative accounts. Instead, it focuses on the importance of such events.

- The Koran is divided into 114 *suras,* or chapters. These are not organized by time but by length, beginning with the longest and working toward the shortest prayers.

- Christians, Jews, and Muslims all lived together peacefully, if not always happily, in the Middle East before the time of the Crusades. As can be seen in "The Prior Who Became a Moslem," Christians and Muslims came into daily contact with one another.

- Omar Khayyam's *Rubaiyat* consists of about 104-line poems on the themes of love and the enjoyment of pleasures from food to drink.

- Omar Khayyam was much better known in his own day as a mathematician and also an astronomer than he was as a poet. His fame in the West comes as the result of a nineteenth-century translation of his works into English.

Excerpt from The Koran

Chapter 48: Victory

*We have given you [Muhammad] a glorious victory [the taking of Mecca, a.d. 630, or of Khaybar a year earlier], so that **God** may forgive you your past and future sins, and perfect His goodness to you; that He may guide you to a straight path and bestow on you His mighty help.*

God: The God of Islam, Allah.

*It was He who sent down **tranquility** into the hearts of the faithful, so that their faith might grow stronger. God's are the **legions** of the heavens and the earth. God is all-knowing and wise.*

*He has caused you to do as you have done, that He may bring the believers, both men and women, into gardens watered by running streams, there to **abide** for ever; that He may forgive them their sins … ; and that He may punish the **hypocrites** and the **idolaters**… who think evil thoughts about God. A turn of evil shall **befall** them, for God is angry with them. He has laid on them his curse and prepared for them the fire of Hell.…*

God's are the legions of the heavens and the earth. God is mighty and wise.

*Those that swear **fealty** to you, swear fealty to God Himself.… He that breaks his **oath** breaks it at his own **peril**, but he that keeps his pledge to God shall be richly rewarded by Him.…*

*Say to the desert Arabs who stay behind: "You shall be called upon to fight a mighty nation, unless they **embrace** Islam. If you prove obedient, God will reward you well. But if you run away, … He will **inflict** on you a stern **chastisement**.…"*

*God was well pleased with the faithful when they swore **allegiance** to you under the tree. He knew what was in their hearts. Therefore he sent down tranquility upon them, and rewarded them with a speedy victory and with the many **spoils** which they have taken.…*

*God has … **stayed** your enemies' hands, so that He may make your victory a sign to true believers and guide you along a straight path.*

It was He who ended hostilities between you in the Valley of Mecca after He had given you victory over them.…

*Those were the **unbelievers** who **debarred** you from the Sacred **Mosque** and prevented your offerings from reaching their destination. But for the fear that you might have trampled underfoot believing men and women unknown to you and thus **incurred** unwitting guilt on their account, God would have commanded you to fight it out with them; but He **ordained** it thus that He might bring whom He will into His mercy. Had the faithful stood apart from them, We would have sternly punished the unbelievers.*

*God has in all truth fulfilled his **apostle's** vision.…*

Tranquility: Peacefulness.

Legions: Large numbers of people.

Abide: Live.

Hypocrites: People who do not act as they preach.

Idolaters: Worshipers of idols, or false gods.

Befall: Happen to.

Fealty: Loyalty.

Oath: Promise.

Peril: Danger, risk.

Embrace: Accept.

Inflict: Impose; cause to suffer.

Chastisement: Punishment; reprimand.

Allegiance: Loyalty.

Spoils: Property or loot taken in war.

Stayed: Stopped.

Unbelievers: In this case, non-Muslims, probably Christians.

Debarred: Excluded.

Mosque: Muslim church; in this case, probably al-Aqsa Mosque in Jerusalem.

Incurred: Brought about; subjected oneself to.

Ordained: Officially ordered.

Apostle: An enthusiastic supporter.

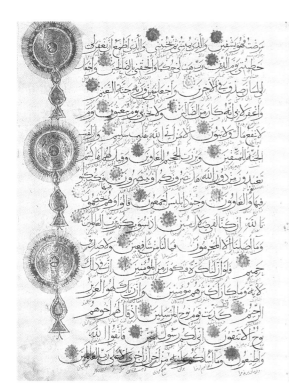
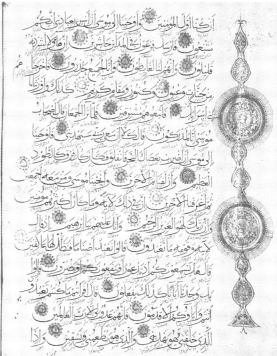

It is He who has sent forth His apostle with guidance and the true Faith, so that he may exalt it above all religions....

Muhammad is God's apostle. Those who follow him are ruthless to the unbelievers but merciful to one another. You see them adoring on their knees, seeking the grace of God and His good will. Their marks are on their faces, the traces of their **prostrations**. Thus are they described in the **Torah** and in the **Gospels**: they are like the seed which puts forth its **shoot** and strengthens it, so that it rises stout and firm upon its stalk, delighting the **sowers**. Through them He seeks to enrage the unbelievers. Yet to those of them who will embrace the Faith and do good works God has promised forgiveness and a rich reward.

Excerpt from "The Holy Light"

The following is a description of the Holy Light, which descends upon the Holy Sepulchre, as the Lord **vouchsafed** to show it to me, his wicked and unworthy servant.... Many pilgrims relate incorrectly the details about the descent of that Holy Light. Some say that the **Holy Ghost** descends upon the Holy Sepulchre in the form of a dove;

Pages of the Koran marking the points for prostration, or prayer. *Museum of the Holy Masumeh Shrine, Qom, Iran/Bridgeman Art Library. Reproduced by permission.*

Prostrations: Acts of lying down with the face downward.

Torah: One of the holy books of Judaism.

Gospels: The teachings of Christ in the first four books of the New Testament of the Bible.

Shoot: An immature plant stem.

Sowers: Planters.

others that it is lightning from heaven which **kindles** the lamps above the Sepulchre of the Lord. This is all untrue, for neither dove nor lightning is to be seen at that moment; but the **Divine** grace comes down unseen from heaven, and lights the lamps of the Sepulchre of our Lord.... On **Holy Friday**, after **Vespers**, they clean the Holy Sepulchre and wash all the lamps that are there; they fill the lamps with pure oil without water and after having put in the **wicks**, leave them unlighted; they **affix** the seals to the Tomb at the second hour of the night. At the same time they **extinguish** all the lamps and wax candles in every church in Jerusalem. Upon that same Friday, at the first hour of the day, I, the unworthy, entered the presence of Prince Baldwin, and bowed myself to the ground before him. Seeing me, as I bowed, he bade me, in a friendly manner, come to him, and said, "What **dost thou** want, Russian **abbot**?" for he knew me and liked me, being a man of great kindness and humility.... I said to him, "My prince and my lord! For the love of God, and out of regard for the Russian princes, allow me to place my lamp on the Holy Sepulchre in the name of the whole Russian country." Then with peculiar kindness and attention he gave me permission to place my lamp on the Sepulchre of the Lord, and sent one of his chief **retainers** with me to the custodian of the Resurrection, and to the keeper of the keys of the Holy Sepulchre.... Opening the sacred portal for me, he ordered me to take off my shoes; and then, having admitted me barefooted to the Holy Sepulchre, with the lamp that I bore, he directed me to place it on the Tomb of the Lord. I placed it, with my sinful hands, on the spot occupied by the sacred feet of our Lord Jesus Christ.... After having placed my lamp on the Holy Sepulchre, and after having adored and kissed, with **penitence** and **pious** tears, the sacred place upon which the body of our Lord Jesus Christ lay; I left the Holy Tomb filled with joy, and retired to my **cell**.

On the **morrow**, Holy Saturday, at the sixth hour of the day, everyone assembles in front of the Church of the Holy Resurrection; foreigners and natives people from all countries, from Babylon, from Egypt, and from every part of the world, come together on that day in countless numbers; the crowd fills the open space round the church and round the place of the Crucifixion. The crush is terrible, and the **turmoil** so great that many persons are **suffocated** in the dense crowd of people who stand, unlighted **tapers** in hand, waiting for the opening of the church doors. The priests alone are inside the church, and priests and crowd alike wait for the arrival of the Prince and his **suite**; then, the doors being opened, the people rush in, pushing and jostling each other, and fill the church and the galleries,

Vouchsafed: Granted, allowed.

Holy Ghost: Also known as the Holy Spirit.

Kindles: Lights, sets ablaze.

Divine: Godly.

Holy Friday: The Friday before Easter Sunday, also called Good Friday.

Vespers: Evening prayer.

Wicks: The strips of material that burn in a candle or oil lamp.

Affix: Fasten, attach.

Extinguish: Put out.

Dost Thou: Do you.

Abbot: The head of a religious abbey or institution for monks.

Retainers: Servants.

Penitence: Regret for a sin.

Pious: Very religious.

Cell: Simple lodging for a monk.

Morrow: Next day.

Turmoil: Disturbance, confusion.

Suffocated: Choked from a lack of air.

Tapers: Candles.

Suite: Attendants or followers.

for the church alone could not contain such a multitude. A large portion of the crowd has to remain outside round **Golgotha** and the place of the skull, and as far as the spot where the crosses were set up; every place is filled with an innumerable multitude.... The faithful shed **torrents** of tears; even he who has a heart of stone cannot refrain from **weeping**; each one, searching the innermost depths of his soul, thinks of his sins, and says secretly to himself, "Will my sins prevent the descent of the Holy Light?" … At the end of the ninth hour, … a small cloud, coming suddenly from the east, rested above the open dome of the church; fine rain fell on the Holy Sepulchre, and wet us and all those who were above the Tomb. It was at this moment that the Holy Light suddenly illuminated the Holy Sepulchre, shining with an awe-aspiring and splendid brightness....

This Holy Light is like no ordinary flame, for it burns in a marvellous way with indescribable brightness, and a **ruddy** colour like that of **cinnabar** . All the people remain standing with lighted tapers, and repeat in a loud voice with intense joy and eagerness: "Lord, have mercy upon us!" …

A leaf from a Koran written in Kufic script during the Abbasid dynasty. © *Werner Forman/Art Resource, NY. Reproduced by permission.*

Golgotha: The place where Christ was crucified.

Torrents: Fast-moving streams of water.

Weeping: Crying.

Ruddy: Reddish.

Cinnabar: A bright red mineral.

The Church of the Holy Sepulchre in Jerusalem is believed to be built on the site of Jesus Christ's tomb.
© *Carmen Redondo/Corbis. Reproduced by permission.*

Kyrie Eleison: Greek for "Lord have mercy," a prayer said at a Catholic mass or religious service.

Prior: Church official or elder.

Monkery: Another word for monastery.

Diligence: Care.

Adoration: Worshiping.

*Directly the light shone in the Holy Sepulchre the chant ceased, and all, crying out "**Kyrie Eleison**," moved towards the church with great joy, bearing the lighted tapers in their hands, and protecting them from the wind. Everyone then goes home.... Carrying the lighted tapers, we returned to our monastery with the abbot and the monks; we finished the Vespers there and then retired to our cells.*

Excerpt from
"The Prior Who Became a Moslem"

*Said Abu Bakr Mohammed ibn Al-Anbari: "I once left Anbar on a journey to 'Amuriyah, where there came out to me the **prior** of the monastery and superior of the **monkery**, called Abd al-Masih, and brought me into the building. There I found forty religious, who entertained me that night with fair guest rite, [ceremony] and I left them after seeing among them such **diligence** in **adoration** and devotion as I never beheld the like of in any others....*

A Christian worshipper lights candles at the Church of the Holy Sepulchre in Jerusalem. It is at this site that Abbot Daniel supposedly witnessed the Holy Light. © *Reuters/Corbis. Reproduced by permission.*

*And next year I made pilgrimage to Meccah and as I was **circumambulating** the Holy House I saw Abd al-Masih the monk also **compassing** the **Ka'abah**, and with him five of his fellows, the **shavelings**. Now when I was sure that it was indeed he, I **accosted** him, saying, 'Are you not Abd al-Masih, the Religious?' and he replied, 'Nay, I am Abdallah, the Desirous.'*

*__Therewith__ I fell to kissing his grey hairs and shedding tears; then, taking him by the hand, I led him aside into a corner of the Temple and said to him, 'Tell me the cause of your conversion to al-Islam;' and he made reply, '**Verily**, it was a wonder of wonders, and **befell** thus:*

*A company of **Moslem devotees** came to the village wherein is our convent, and sent a youth to buy them food. He saw, in the market, a Christian **damsel** selling bread, who was of the **fairest** of women; and he was struck at first sight with such love of her, that his senses failed him and he fell on his face in a fainting fit. When he **revived**, he returned to his companions and told them what had befallen him, saying, 'Go you about your business; I may not go with you.'*

*They **chided** him and **exhorted** him, but he paid no **heed** to them; so they left him while he entered the village and seated himself at the door of the woman's booth. She asked him what he wanted, and he told her that he was in love with her, whereupon she turned from him; but he **abode** in his place three days without tasting food, keeping his eyes fixed on her face. Now when as she saw that he departed not from her, she went to her people and **acquainted** them with his case, and they set on him the village boys, who stoned him and bruised his ribs and broke his head; but, for all this, he would not budge.*

*Then the villagers took counsel together to **slay** him; but a man of them came to me and told me of his case, and I went out to him and found him lying **prostrate** on the ground. So I wiped the blood from his face and carried him to the convent, and dressed his wounds; and there he abode with me fourteen days. But as soon as he could walk, he left the monastery and returned to the door of the woman's booth, where he sat gazing on her as before.*

When she saw him she came out to him and said, 'By Allah you move me to pity! Will you enter my faith that I may marry you?'

He cried, 'Allah forbid that I should put off the faith of Unity and enter that of Plurality!'

Circumambulating: Walking around.

Compassing: Going around.

Ka'abah: The central stone structure of the Great Mosque or church in Mecca.

Shavelings: Persons with a shaved head for religious purposes.

Accosted: Greeted.

Therewith: After that.

Verily: Truly.

Befell: Happened.

Moslem: Muslim.

Devotees: Believers.

Damsel: Young woman.

Fairest: Prettiest.

Revived: Recovered.

Chided: Scolded.

Exhorted: Encouraged.

Heed: Attention.

Abode: Stayed; remained.

Acquainted: Told, made familiar with.

Slay: Kill.

Prostrate: Stretched out with the face down.

The TEMPLE of MECCA.

Said she, 'Come in with me to my house and take your will of me and go your way in peace.'

Said he, 'Not so, I will not waste the worship of twelve years for the **lust** of an eye-twinkle.'

Said she, 'Then depart from me **forthwith**;' and he said, 'My heart will not suffer me to do that'; whereupon she turned her **countenance** from him.

Presently the boys found him out and began to **pelt** him with stones; and he fell on his face, saying, 'Verily, Allah is my protector, who sent down the Book of the **Koran**; and He protects the Righteous!'

At this I **sallied forth** and driving away the boys, lifted his head from the ground and heard him say, 'Allah mine, unite me with her in Paradise!'

Then I carried him to the monastery, but he died, before I could reach it, and I bore him **without** the village and I dug for him a grave and buried him.

An engraving of the Great Mosque in the city of Mecca that is described in "The Prior Who Became a Moslem." © *Hulton-Deutsch Collection/Corbis. Reproduced by permission.*

Lust: Passion.

Forthwith: Immediately.

Countenance: Face, features.

Pelt: Hit.

Koran: Muslim holy book.

Sallied Forth: Set out or moved quickly.

Without: Outside.

And next night when half of it was spent, the damsel cried with a great cry (and she in her bed); so the villagers flocked to her and questioned her of her case.

Said she, 'As I slept, behold the Moslem man came in to me and taking me by the hand, carried me to the gate of Paradise; but the Guardian denied me entrance, saying, 'It is forbidden to unbelievers.'

*So I embraced Al Islam at his hands and, entering with him, beheld therein **pavilions** and trees, such as I cannot describe to you. Moreover, he brought me to a pavilion of jewels and said to me, 'Of a truth this is my pavilion and yours, nor will I enter it except with you; after five nights you shall be with me therein, if it be the will of Allah Almighty.'*

Then he put forth his hand to a tree which grew at the door of the pavilion and plucked there from two apples and gave them to me, saying, 'Eat this and keep the other, that the monks may see it.'

*So I ate one of them and never tasted I any sweeter. Then he took my hand and **fared forth** and carried me back to my house; and, when I awoke, I found the taste of the apple in my mouth and the other in my hand.'*

*So saying she brought out the apple, and in the darkness of the night it shone as it were a sparkling star. So they carried her (and the apple with her) to the monastery, where she repeated her vision and showed it to us; never saw we its like among all the fruits of the world. Then I took a knife and cut the apple into pieces according as we were folk in company; and never knew we any more delicious than its **savour** nor more delightsome than its scent; but we said, '**Haply** this was a devil that appeared unto her to **seduce** her from her faith.'*

*Thereupon her people took her and went away; but she **abstained** from eating and drinking and on the fifth night she rose*

Sir Richard Burton who translated *The Arabian Nights,* which includes "The Prior Who Became a Moslem." *Photograph courtesy of The Library of Congress.*

Pavilions: Decorative summerhouses or structures open to the air.

Fared Forth: Traveled or went out.

Savour: Flavor.

Haply: By chance.

Seduce: Lead in the wrong direction.

Abstained: Refused to do something.

from her bed, and going forth the village to the grave of her Moslem lover threw herself upon it and died, her family not knowing what was come of her. But, on the **morrow**, there came to the village two Moslem elders, **clad** in hair cloth, and with them two women in like garb, and said, 'O people of the village, with you is a woman Saint, a Waliyah of the friends of Allah, who died a **Moslemah**; and we will take charge of her **in lieu** of you.'

So the villagers sought her and found her dead on the Moslem's grave; and they said, 'This was one of us and she died in our faith; so we will take charge of her.'

Rejoined the two old men, '**Nay**, she died a Moslemah and we claim her.'

And the dispute grew to a quarrel between them, till one of the **Shaykhs** said, 'Be this the test of her faith: the forty monks of the monastery shall come and try to lift her from the grave. If they succeed, then she died a **Nazarene**; if not, one of us shall come and lift her up and if she be lifted by him, she died a Moslemah.'

The villagers agreed to this and fetched the forty monks, who heartened one another, and came to her to lift her, but could not. Then we tied a great rope round her middle and **haled** at it; but the rope broke **in sunder**, and she stirred not; and the villagers came and did the like, but could not move her from her place.

At last, when all means failed, we said to one of the two Shaykhs, 'Come and lift her.'

So he went up to the grave and, covering her with his **mantle**, said, 'In the name of Allah the Compassionating, the Compassionate, and of the Faith of the Apostle of Allah, on whom be prayers and peace!' Then he lifted her and, taking her in his **bosom**, **betook** himself with her to a cave hard by, where they laid her, and the two women came and washed her and **shrouded** her. Then the two elders bore her to her Moslem lover's grave and prayed over her and buried her by his side and went their ways.

Now we were eye witnesses of all this; and, when we were alone with one another, we said, '**In sooth**, the truth is most worthy to be followed;' and indeed the truth has been made **manifest** to us, nor is there a proof more **patent** of the truth of **al-Islam** than that we have seen this day with our eyes.'

So I and all the monks became Moslems and likewise did the villagers; and we sent to the people of **Mesopotamia** for a doctor of

Morrow: The next day.

Clad: Dressed.

Moslemah: Muslim woman.

In Lieu: Instead.

Rejoined: Replied.

Nay: No.

Shaykhs: Arab or Muslim leaders, also spelled sheikh.

Nazarene: A Christian.

Haled: Pulled.

In Sunder: In pieces.

Mantle: Coat or cloak.

Bosom: Chest.

Betook: Went to.

Shrouded: Wrapped for burial.

In Sooth: Truly.

Manifest: Clear, evident.

Patent: Recognizable, obvious.

Al-Islam: The Islamic faith.

Mesopotamia: Modern-day Iraq.

the law, to instruct us in the **ordinances** of al-Islam and the **canons** of the Faith. They sent us a learned man and a pious, who taught us the rites of prayer and the **tenets** of the faith; and we are now in ease **abounding**; so to Allah be the praise and the thanks!"

Excerpt: "Profession of Faith"

*Ye, who seek for **pious** fame,*

*And that light should **gild** your name,*

*Be this duty **ne'er** forgot—*

Love your neighbor—harm him not.

To Thee, Great Spirit, I appeal,

Who can'st the gates of truth unseal;

I follow none, nor ask the way

*Of men who go, like me, **astray**;*

*They **perish**, but Thou can'st not die,*

But liv'st to all eternity.

*Such is **vain** man's uncertain state,*

*A little makes him **base** or great;*

*One hand shall hold the **Koran's scroll**,*

The other raise the sparkling bowl—

*One saves, and one **condemns** the soul.*

The temple I frequent is high,

A turkish-vaulted dome—the sky,

That spans the world with majesty.

*Not quite a Muslim is my **creed**,*

*Nor quite a **Giaour**; my faith indeed*

May startle some who hear me say,

I'd give my pilgrim staff away,

*And sell my **turban**, for an hour*

*Of music in a fair one's **bower**.*

*I'd sell the **rosary** for wine,*

*Though holy names around it **twine**.*

Ordinances: Laws.

Canons: Major principles or laws of a religion.

Tenets: Central beliefs.

Abounding: Having in large numbers.

Pious: Devoutly religious.

Gild: To apply a thin gold covering.

Ne'er: Never.

Astray: On the wrong path or direction.

Perish: Die.

Vain: Being concerned with appearances.

Base: Without principles or morals.

Koran: Islamic holy book.

Scroll: A roll of paper with printing on it.

Condemns: Finds guilty or unfit.

Creed: Belief.

Giaour: A non-Muslim, especially a Christian.

Turban: A Muslim headdress.

Bower: A comfortable, shady place under a tree.

Rosary: In the Catholic faith, a string of beads for counting prayers.

Twine: Interlace, twist.

And prayers the pious make so long

Are turned by me to joyous song;

Or, if a prayer I should repeat,

It is at my beloved's feet.

They blame me that my words are clear;

Because I am not what I appear;

*Nor do my acts my words **belie**—*

*At least, I **shun** hypocrisy.*

It happened that but yesterday

*I marked a **potter** beating clay.*

*The earth spoke out— "Why **dost thou** strike?*

Both thou and I are born alike;

*Though some may sink and some may **soar**,*

We all are earth, and nothing more."

Belie: Show to be false.

Shun: Ignore, reject.

Potter: A person who makes clay pots.

Dost Thou: Do you.

Soar: Fly up high in the air.

What happened next…

While the view of writers such as Omar Khayyam about religion and private faith was in the minority in the Middle Ages, such a perspective became more and more common after the age of the Crusades. The power of reason over faith, of objective thought over blind belief, increased through the centuries of the Renaissance and Enlightenment, from the fourteenth to the eighteenth centuries. A belief in science also competed against a belief in religions until, by the nineteenth century, the German philosopher Friedrich Nietzsche could declare, "God is dead." However, science and industrial progress came into question in the twentieth century, a time that suffered from the threat of global destruction from atomic and hydrogen bombs and from pollution, all the by-products of science and rationalism. In the twenty-first century, religion is once again on the rise in many countries, with nineteen major religions and two hundred and

Too Earthy for Publication

Both the *Rubaiyat* of Omar Khayyam and the *Book of a Thousand Nights and a Night* gained their most important translations by nineteenth-century Englishmen. Edward Fitzgerald (1809–83), lived a secluded and private life in the English countryside. His first translation of *The Rubaiyat of Omar Khayyam* appeared in 1859; with later editions supported by famous poets and artists of the day, the book became an instant classic, appealing to the Victorian, or late-nineteenth-century, English taste with its advice that humankind should live life to the fullest, for we do not know what to expect after death.

Sir Richard Francis Burton, translator of *The Arabian Nights,* was born in 1820 and died in 1890. He was, however, a polar opposite to Fitzgerald, leading an exciting, adventurous life, exploring in Africa and South America. An expert in many languages, he was also a busy writer. Late in life he took on the translation of the *Arabian Nights,* which he published in sixteen volumes in 1885.

Both of these books deal with earthy themes: drinking, making love, and generally having the type of fun that was not always considered proper. Many of the poems and tales of both books were hidden away until the twentieth century. Some critics still complain that parts of the *Rubaiyat* and of the *Arabian Nights,* are not fit for children to read. Others say that the content of the English editions of these books owe as much to the outlook of their translators as they do to the original author or authors.

seventy different identified large religious groups. Only about 13 percent of the world's population identified itself as non-religious in the year 2000, according to one study. With this return to religion comes, unfortunately, the concept of holy war, which is once again a fact of life.

Did you know...

- Because of the prohibition of translating the Koran, it has become one of the widest-read books in its original language, rivaling even blockbuster novels of the modern day.

- Modern Islam now has 1.2 billion worshippers worldwide, or about one-fifth of the world's population. Christianity, at the same time, has more than two billion followers, representing about a third of the global population. Amazingly, Christians are divided into about thirty-four thousand separate groups.

- Performing miracles, such as that of the Holy Fire, or Holy Light, in Jerusalem, is required for a person to become a saint in the Catholic Church. The first step is beatification, in which a person is called "blessed" by the church. To be beatified, two miracles associated with that person must be proved by the church. The next step is canonization, or becoming a saint. This process used to be like a trial, in which the person proposed for sainthood had his or her life looked into thoroughly. But without miracles, there would be no saints.

- The organizing device or trick of *The Arabian Nights* is that all the stories are told by Scheherezade, or Sheherazade, to keep her husband, King Shahryar (or Schriyar), from killing her. So she must entertain him with a story each night for one thousand and one nights.

- Conversion, or changing religions, as seen in "The Prior Who Became a Moslem," did not always happen as a result of an honest change of faith. During the time of the Crusades, prisoners of one side or another could buy their freedom by converting to one religion or another. The most famous attempted conversion during the Crusades was that of the Egyptian sultan al-Malik al-Kamil by Saint Francis of Assisi during the Fifth Crusade in 1219. Francis went to Egypt hoping to end the fighting by persuading the sultan to become a Christian. Instead, Francis had a month-long discussion with the sultan, during which the sultan tried to get Francis to convert to Islam.

Consider the following...
- Discuss some of the similarities and differences between Christianity and the Muslim faith.

- How is the personal faith of Omar Khayyam, as shown in the excerpted poem, different from that of formal religions?

- Explain the effect the Crusades had on modern relations between the West and the Middle East.

For More Information

Books

Abbot Daniel. *The Pilgrimage of the Russian Abbot Daniel in the Holy Land, 1106–1107.* Edited by C. W. Wilson. London: Palestine Pilgrims' Text Society, 1888.

Burton, Sir Richard Francis. *Arabian Nights.* Edited by Bennet Cerf. New York: Random House/Modern Library, 1997.

Horne, Charles F., ed. *The Sacred Books and Early Literature of the East.* New York: Parke, Austin, and Lipscomb, 1917.

The Koran. Translated by N. J. Dawood. London: Penguin Books, 1990.

Web Sites

Abbot Daniel. "The Holy Light; How It Descends upon the Holy Sepulchre." *The Pilgrimage of the Russian Abbot Daniel in the Holy Land 1106–1107 A.D.* http://www.holyfire.org/eng/doc_Daniil.htm (accessed on August 4, 2004).

"Alf Layla wa Layla (A Thousand Nights and a Night)." *Electronic Literature Foundation.* http://www.arabiannights.org/index2.html (accessed on August 4, 2004).

"Islam during the Crusades." *The ORB: On-line Reference Book for Medieval Studies.* http://the-orb.net/textbooks/crusade/islam.html (accessed on August 4, 2004).

Omar Khayyam. "Profession of Faith, c. 1120." *Internet Medieval Sourcebook.* http://www.fordham.edu/halsall/source/omarkhayyam-faith.html (accessed August 4, 2004).

"The Prior Who Became a Moslem." *The Arabian Nights: Excerpts from Tales on Christianity and the Crusades.* http://ksumail.kennesaw.edu/~bstevens/Burton.html (accessed on August 4, 2004).

Using the Faith

Excerpt from "The Saladin Tithe" (1188)

Original declaration of Henry II, King of England; Reprinted in *Source Book for Medieval Economic History;* **Edited by Roy C. Cave and Herbert H. Coulson; Published in 1965**

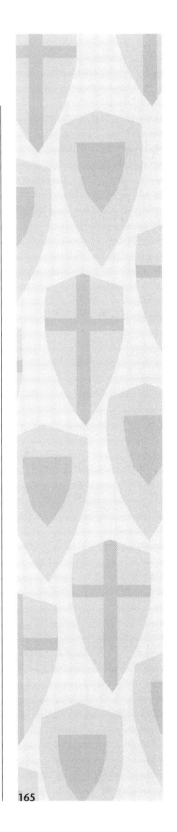

Religious faith was put to powerful use during the two hundred years of the Crusades. Time and again, faithful Christians and Muslims were called to arms to fight for their god. Over and over, the inhabitants of Europe and the Middle East were asked by their spiritual leaders to put their private lives on hold and risk all for a matter of faith: control of the Holy Land and the sites in Jerusalem that are sacred to both religions.

Raising an army is not a simple process. Strong preachers were needed on both sides to fire up the people, to fill them with enthusiasm for a holy war. But when the soldiers were gathered, there came the question of who would pay to feed and arm these forces, which were often forty thousand to fifty thousand strong. With the First Crusade (1095–99), Crusaders were expected to pay their own way to the Holy Land and be able to support themselves while there. But such was the enthusiasm for a holy war that armies of common people and poor farmers also set off for Constantinople in 1096, following the powerful preacher Peter the Hermit. These people expected to survive on the

An engraving on King Henry II's tomb. King Henry of England wrote the declaration implementing the Saladin Tithe in order to pay for the Crusades. © *Bettmann/ Corbis. Reproduced by permission.*

goods and property that they could seize from people they conquered in battle. Thus many Crusades started close to home with actions against the Jews. Christians believed that the call for Crusades often legitimized, or made lawful, stealing from the European Jews.

Nobles who set off on the Crusades often sold part of their holdings, or lands, to finance the cost of their own travels and that of the men they brought with them. Richard I, the Lionheart, of England supposedly said that he would sell off all of London to finance his trip during the Third Crusade (1189–92) if he could find a buyer. By 1165 the king of France promised to give a small percentage of his annual income to help fund Crusades and asked the noblemen of his kingdom to do the same. This money was collected by the local, or parish, priest and kept in a huge chest. This practice continued to spread, and in 1185 the king of England was also issuing such a tax. When both the kings of England and France agreed to go on a Crusade in 1188, they decided to put another tax on all those people who did not go to the Crusade to regain Jerusalem from the Muslim leader, Saladin, who had taken the city in 1187. Called the Saladin Tithe, this payment was set at 10 percent of a person's annual income, the highest tax ever laid on the people of these kingdoms. In the following excerpt from the declaration of King Henry II of England, we see exactly who paid this tithe and how much, as well as who was excused from it.

Things to remember while reading the excerpt from "Using the Faith":

- The church also raised money for the Crusades by taxing its own clergy, or those ordained to lead religious services. For the Fourth Crusade (1202–04) Pope Innocent III had the clergy pay a fortieth of their yearly income. The bill continued to rise for the clergy, too, reaching a twentieth of their income by the late thirteenth century.

- Muslims also pay a tithe, or religious tax, but in Islam this is called the *zakat* and is one of the five pillars, or main principles, of their faith. This tithe is set between 2 and 3 percent of a person's annual income and is meant to help support the poor and establish social justice and equality throughout Islam.

- Tax collectors were needed for such tithes, and at first this duty fell to the Christian clergy. But soon, other groups took over the job. Two military religious orders were founded in the Holy Land early in the twelfth century, the Knights Hospitallers in 1113 and the Knights Templar in 1118. To begin with, these religious orders helped Christians in the Holy Land, either in hospitals or by securing their travel to pilgrimage sites. But these functions quickly grew when the church recognized the orders and approved of their role as elite monk-soldiers defending the Holy Land. The Teutonic Knights were added to these groups later, and together the three orders became the professional soldiers of the Holy Land. But they also had a less military role: the Templars and the Hospitallers both helped collect tithes in Europe in 1185 and 1188.

- The Templars and Hospitallers were supported by alms, or charitable money given by the church and nobles. Both orders soon became wealthy. They were then able to establish institutions all over Europe and the Holy Land.

- The famous Catholic scholar of the twelfth century, Bernard of Clairvaux, laid out the rules and regulations of the Knights Templar order. He attempted to clearly define what the Templars could and could not do, from dress to manner of prayer. He also made an excuse for al-

Le gran richeses, ge dedens troueron.
Le riches pailes, li uar li siglaton.
Li or largent, li peires li carbon.
Baudoz tenoit au poing son copaignon.
Amis dist il, tot ast resor uos don.

An illuminated manuscript of a knight traveling with a chest containing collected tithes in order to finance the Crusades. © *Archivo Iconografico, S.A./Corbis. Reproduced by permission.*

lowing such religious men to kill, something that the Christian Ten Commandments seems to disapprove of. In his treatise, or policy statement, "In Praise of the New Knighthood," Bernard made the distinction between "homicide," killing another human, and "malicide," killing evil itself. Clearly, for Bernard and the church, killing Muslims in the name of God did not go against church doctrine.

Excerpt from "The Saladin Tithe"

1. Each person will give in charity one tenth of his rents and movable goods for the taking of the land of Jerusalem; except for the arms, horses, and clothing of knights, and likewise for the hors-

es, books, clothing, and **vestments**, and church furniture of the clergy, and except for precious stones belonging to the clergy or the **laity**.

2. Let the money be collected in every **parish** in the presence of the parish priest and of the rural **dean**, and of one **Templar** and one **Hospitaller**, and of a servant of the Lord King and a clerk of the King, and of a servant of a baron and his clerk, and the clerk of the bishop; and let the archbishops, bishops, and deans in every parish **excommunicate** every one who does not pay the lawful **tithe**, in the presence of, and to the certain knowledge of, those who, as has been said above, ought to be present. And if any one according to the knowledge of those men give less than he should, let there be elected from the parish four or six lawful men, who shall say on **oath** what is the quantity that he ought to have declared; then it shall be reasonable to add to his payment what he failed to give.

3. But the clergy and knights who have **taken the cross**, shall give none of that tithe except from their own goods and the property of their lord; and whatever their men owe shall be collected for their use by the above and returned **intact** to them.

4. Moreover, the bishops in every parish of their **sees** shall cause to be announced by their letters on Christmas Day and on the **Feast of St. Stephen**, and on the **Feast of St. John**, that each will collect the said tithe into his own hands before the **Feast of the Purification of the Blessed Virgin** and, on the following day and afterwards, each will pay, in the presence of those who have been mentioned, at the place to which he has been **summoned**.

What happened next...

The amount earned by the Saladin Tithe was quite large for its day, more than seventy thousand pounds, or close to $100 million. But it was so unpopular among the nobles that the kings of France and of England had to promise never again to set such a high tax, and they kept their word. In the future such taxes were kept at levels of about 5 percent at the highest. One thing such taxes as the Saladin Tithe proved, though, was that the secular, or nonreligious, powers

Vestments: Religious robes.

Laity: Lay people, or worshippers, as opposed to the clergy, or preachers.

Parish: Church administrative district.

Dean: Local church official.

Templar: Religious military order, the Knights Templars.

Hospitaller: Religious military order, the Knights Hospitallers.

Excommunicate: Expel from the church.

Tithe: A religious tax, usually one-tenth of annual earnings.

Oath: A sworn promise to tell the truth.

Taken the Cross: Agreed to go on Crusade.

Intact: Unused, whole.

Sees: Larger administrative districts for the church.

Feast of St. Stephen: Holy day in the Catholic Church, December 26.

Feast of St. John: Holy day in the Catholic Church, June 22–23.

Feast of the Purification of the Blessed Virgin: Holy day in the Catholic Church, February 2.

Summoned: Called to be present.

German Fighting Monks

The Knights Templar was one of several military orders founded during the Crusades. The other main orders were the Knights Hospitallers and the Teutonic Knights, or the Teutonic Order, founded in 1190. Like the Hospitallers, the Teutonic Knights grew out of an order of monks, or religious men, who served at a hospital in Jerusalem. The Hospital of Saint Mary of the Teutons served mostly German crusaders. When it became a fighting order, Teutonic Knights' members took the usual vow of monks: poverty, chastity, and obedience.

Unlike the two other orders, however, the Teutonic Knights played a role not only in defending the Holy Land but also in bringing central and eastern Europe under the thumb of the church. They were forced into this role because the other two orders were so well organized in the Holy Land and there was little room for the Teutonic

of Europe were able to raise vast sums by this method of taxation. Up to the eleventh century only the church had been able to collect money from the faithful through such tithing, but the nobles had not yet done so. The Crusades provided an emergency situation, though, and the kings of Europe took advantage of it to begin a required tax for a specific purpose. Such a system ultimately led to the modern income tax that people all over the world groan about at tax time.

The Knights Templars became bound up in financing the Crusades when they acted as middlemen in Crusader banking or money transfers from Europe to the Holy Land. Crusaders could deposit their money in Europe with a Templar house and then receive credit for it from Templars in the Holy Land when they arrived there. This system is similar to modern-day travelers checks. This system of credit was important, as many Crusaders were robbed on their way to the Holy Land or lost their funds in shipwrecks en route. The Knights Templars also continued to play an important role in the defense of the Crusader states in the Holy Land, respected by friends and enemies alike. However, the rivalry that grew between them, the Hospitallers, and the Teutonic Knights was partly responsible for the weakening of the Crusader states and their inability to come together to fight their

Knights to grow there. In Europe they fought non-Christians and also breakaway Christian groups. In Transylvania they battled a tribe called the Cumans in the service of Andrew II of Hungary. They also helped defeat tribes in land that is now northern Germany and the Baltic states, bringing them under Christian rule for a Polish duke. The Teutonic Order was centered in Germany and had a strong central administration. This, in turn, helped lay the foundation for the Prussian state, which ultimately led to modern Germany. The order lost much of its power in the sixteenth century during the Reformation, when the Catholic Church was challenged by the new Protestant Church in Prussia. The Teutonic Knights hung on after that time in the Catholic parts of Germany until the beginning of the nineteenth century. It survived in some parts of Europe into the twenty-first century, but only as a sort of club or honorary order.

common enemy, Islam. The three orders did forget their differences finally, but too late, at the unsuccessful defense of the Crusader city of Acre when it fell to the Muslims in 1291.

This defeat marked the end of the Crusader states in the Holy Land and the Templars, along with the other military orders, retreated from the shores of the eastern Mediterranean Sea. The Templars went to Cyprus, where they gave up their soldiering and focused on banking and money exchange. But as their wealth grew, they gained new enemies, including the king of France, Philip IV, who wanted their wealth to finance a war in Belgium. He arranged for the downfall of the Templars, accusing them of sacrilegious, or nonreligious, behavior. This allowed the king to take the money and property of the Templars. The order was completely destroyed in 1314, and its leader, Jacques de Molay, was burned at the stake for heresy (going against the teachings of the church).

Did you know...

- The system of tithing, or of giving one-tenth of a person's annual crops or income to support the clergy, goes back to ancient times. This was made obligatory, or required, by the Catholic Church in the sixth century.

- Crusading was an expensive business. At the time of the Seventh Crusade (1248–54), Louis IX of France spent close to three million *livres,* a currency of the time. This amount equaled more than twelve times his annual income.

- By the middle of the thirteenth century the pope had gotten out of the business of sponsoring Crusades, leaving it to the kings of Europe, such as Louis IX of France. The church continued to collect money from the faithful for the Crusades, but this was handed over directly to the Crusaders.

- The three military-religious orders that were developed during the Crusades could easily be identified by their uniforms. While the members of the Knights Templars wore a white robe with a red cross on it, the Hospitallers chose a white cross against a black robe; the Teutonic Knights went for a black cross on a white robe.

- Becoming a knight was no easy job. At the age of seven, noble youths became pages, or boy servants, in the castles of other nobles. Then, at about age fourteen, they traded in the short dagger, or knife, of the page for a sword and trained as squires in the apprenticeship, or the service, of other knights, learning the skills of horsemanship and military techniques. After seven years of such training, they were knighted, usually at the age of twenty-one.

- The Crusades were an expensive and tragic time in terms of lives lost as well as money spent. It is difficult to estimate the total number of people who died in the two centuries of ongoing religious wars, but by adding up the body counts from various contemporary accounts of massacres and deaths by disease and in battles from both the Muslim and Christian documents, some historians have calculated that about 1.5 million people died between 1096 and the end of the Crusades in 1291. Of course, by modern-day standards this seems like a low number. Fifty million died in World War II alone. And then there were also the Mongol wars of conquest during the thirteenth century, at the same time as the Crusades.

It is estimated that forty million people were killed as the Mongols built their empire, this at a time when the total world population was estimated to be just four hundred million people.

Consider the following...

- Explain how the Catholic Church tried to finance the Crusades.

- Discuss two financial aspects of the Crusades that led to modern banking and taxing systems.

- What role do you think religion should have in the political life of a nation?

For More Information

Books

Cave, Roy C., and Herbert H. Coulson. *A Source Book for Medieval Economic History.* New York: Biblo and Tannen, 1965.

Zacour, N. P., and H. W. Hazard, eds. *A History of the Crusades,* Volume 6, *The Impact of the Crusades on Europe.* Madison: University of Wisconsin Press, 1989.

Web Sites

Bernard of Clairvaux, "In Praise of the New Knighthood." *ORB.* Available http://the-orb.net/encyclop/religion/monastic/bernard.html (accessed August 4, 2004).

Henry the II. "The Saladin Tithe, 1188." *Internet Medieval Sourcebook.* http://www.fordham.edu/halsall/source/1188Saldtith.html (accessed August 4, 2004).

Text Credits

The editors wish to thank the copyright holders of the excerpted criticism included in this volume and the permissions managers of many book and magazine publishing companies for assisting us in securing reproduction rights. We are also grateful to the staffs of the Detroit Public Library, the Library of Congress, the University of Detroit Mercy Library, Wayne State University Purdy/Kresge Library Complex, and the University of Michigan Libraries for making their resources available to us. Following is a list of the copyright holders who have granted us permission to reproduce material in this volume of *The Crusades: Primary Sources*. Every effort has been made to trace copyright, but if omissions have been made, please let us know.

COPYRIGHTED EXCERPTS IN *THE CRUSADES: PRIMARY SOURCES* WERE REPRODUCED FROM THE FOLLOWING BOOKS:

Al-Abiwardi, Abu l-Musaffar. From *Arab Historians of the Crusades—Selected and Translated from the Arabic*

Index

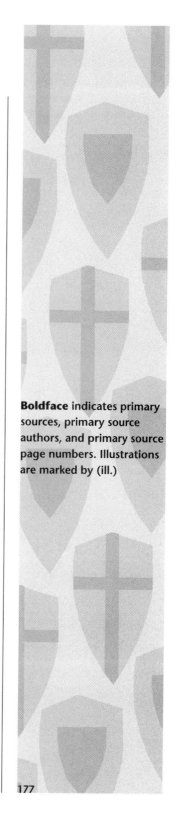

Boldface indicates primary sources, primary source authors, and primary source page numbers. Illustrations are marked by (ill.)